THE
COMPLETE BOOK
OF
PAINT

THE
COMPLETE BOOK
OF
PAINT

A COMPREHENSIVE GUIDE TO PAINT
TECHNIQUES FOR WALLS, FLOORS,
FURNITURE, FABRICS, AND METALWORK

BY DAVID CARTER
TEXT BY CHARLES HEMMING

CLARKSON POTTER/PUBLISHERS
NEW YORK

Published by Clarkson N. Potter/Publishers,
201 East 50th Street, New York, NY 10022.
Member of the Crown Publishing Group.

Random House, Inc. New York, Toronto,
London, Sydney, Auckland
http://www.randomhouse.com/

CLARKSON N. POTTER, POTTER and colophon
are tradmarks of Clarkson N. Potter, Inc.

Originally published in Great Britain by
Conran Octopus Limited in 1996.

Printed in China

Carter, David.
    The Complete Book of Paint / by David Carter
    p. cm
1. House painting—Amateurs' manuals. 2. Wood
finishing—Amateurs' manuals. 3. Furniture painting—Amateurs' manuals. 4. Textile painting—
Amateurs' manuals. I. Title.
TT305.C29   1996 96-1177
698'.1—dc20   CIP

ISBN 0-517-70451-X

10 9 8 7 6 5 4 3 2

First American Edition

Contents

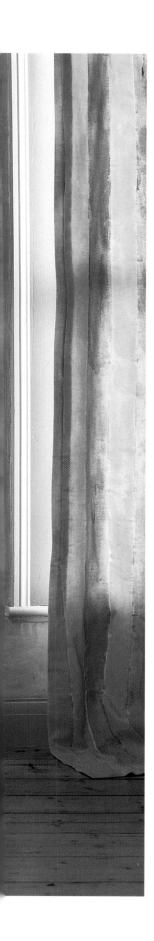

introduction

PAINT IS ONE OF THE QUICKEST AND CHEAPEST ways of transforming your surroundings, and each year thousands of gallons of paint are bought by home decorators. Painting is a skill that once acquired can give lasting pleasure, and many are now discovering that creating a simple, elegant effect takes no more than a little deftness and the mastery of a few basic techniques. With perseverance, even the amateur can aspire to the handiwork of the professional.

The Complete Book of Paint aims to provide a comprehensive guide that takes you through the entire process of painting. It starts with a consideration of the space at your disposal, and the basic principles of selecting and combining colors. This is followed by pages of inspirational photographs, demonstrating how others have dealt with all kinds of different rooms and situations, both inside and outside the home. Next, a comprehensive section on techniques and effects presents the enormous range of options available, from simple flat color on walls and woodwork, to the more elaborate confections of broken-color techniques and trompe l'oeil, explaining how to apply paint in a myriad different ways to all kinds of surfaces, from walls and floors to furniture and metalwork. Then comes a series of specially designed projects from the creative mind of David Carter, incorporating many of the techniques described elsewhere in the book. Many effects are easy to achieve, others a little more intricate and challenging. An extensive directory of paints follows, together with a summary of which paints are best suited to which surface. Finally, the book closes with a practical reference section describing which tools are suitable for specific jobs, how to calculate paint quantities, how to prepare surfaces correctly, and how to mix and tint your own paints.

Paint is so versatile and is available in such an enormous range of
colours and finishes that it can be used to protect and decorate almost
any surface, from wood, plaster and stone, to metal and fabric.

WHETHER YOU ARE DECORATING NEW OR FAMILIAR
SURROUNDINGS, AN UNDERSTANDING OF THE SPACE YOU
ARE DEALING WITH AND THE COLOR OPTIONS AT YOUR
DISPOSAL ARE ESSENTIAL TO ENSURE SUCCESSFUL RESULTS.

space and
color

*PAINT OFFERS AN ENORMOUS VARIETY of color, texture and
pattern. Not only does it enhance and protect the interiors
and exteriors of the buildings in which we live and work, it*
*transforms the way in which we see them so
that even their structures can seem changed.
Depending on how it is used, paint has the ability to make small structures appear larger and
outsized ones less overwhelming, revitalize a
tired and worn surface, or lend a brand-new
object the look of mellowed age.*

*When we consider the diversity of the build-
ings we occupy, to say nothing of the objects
and possessions with which we surround our-
selves, choosing how to decorate and protect
them can be difficult. First, decide on what you
want to achieve, then consider the actual shape of the space
or object to be decorated. How will it be used and when?
Which colors and types of paint will be needed? Once these
basics are determined, everything else will fall into place.*

Strong, well-balanced areas of color can serve as a background to a
whole variety of different objects and textures without the overall effect
appearing disjointed or disorganized.

THE PAINTED SPACE

A light but warm yellow adorns the walls of this tall, sunlit room. The shade balances the strong reds, pinks and blues, preventing them from dominating the room, while they in turn anchor the airy lemon and white of the furnishings. White curtains prevent the green tones of the foliage outside the window turning the yellow "acid."

(RIGHT)

It has been said that there is no such thing as an ugly room, only rooms of different shapes. But all rooms are influenced by their history, their function and their former use. They are also influenced by light, or the lack of it. So before you set out to paint a room, or any other area of a building, it is wise to observe a few simple guidelines.

PERIOD AND FASHION

Architecture is often considered the monarch of the visual arts because all the other categories fit within it or are dominated by it. What is certain is that all buildings are the products of succeeding fashions, each of which mirrored its age.

Some buildings are more versatile than others. A Victorian house with tall bay windows and high rooms can be remarkably flexible in its capacity to take on not only color schemes of its own period, but those of the 1920s and '30s, and even wholly contemporary ideas. On the other hand, a Welsh longhouse with low beams, rough walls and a vast inglenook fireplace will look decidedly peculiar if it is treated to a finish of faux marbling. An Art Deco house with its metal windows and sheer walls would be totally unsuited to craft-revival stencils. Conversely, a featureless modern apartment may be able to carry off an enormous variety of paint effects simply because it is so anonymous.

It would be unwise to state categorically which paint finishes originating in what periods should be used where; if applied with panache and discrimination, opposites can excel together, although this is not

always the case. Domestic interiors are usually eclectic mixtures of many diverse styles, periods and ideas; this is what differentiates them from museums or mere statements of current fashion. However, there are rules which, if ignored, will leave you with visually unfortunate results. For instance, if you wish to paint a building in its original color scheme but you use modern-day paints and paint effects, the colors will overpower the objects and the light will be distorted. Many contemporary colors have a sharper finish than their traditional counterparts, which were generally softer and more muted in tone. However, most modern paints can be doctored to produce period colors and effects using the techniques described in this book.

There is no reason why the atmosphere of a Mexican hacienda or a Roman villa cannot be reproduced in buildings of most periods if you so wish, provided that you are forthright and consistent about it. A kitchen extension can be turned into a Pompeian annex by using an undulating plaster finish, terracotta colorwash, malachite-green lining work at dado, or chair rail, height, antiqued stencils forming a frieze below the ceiling, and by marbling or stippling the floor. As long as the colors are right, such a scheme will fail only if the execution is wrong, or if the logic has not been carried through and another part of the room is treated as 1930s suburbia.

To say that fashion is temporary is a statement of the obvious, but few people can afford the upheaval of changing a painted interior as often as they might alter the style of their clothes. The best guide is to choose paint effects which please and excite you, because if carried out with conviction, they will be recognized as an extension of your own personality and interests, rather than a reflection of someone else's taste. As such, you will feel under no obligation to change your decor until you wish.

FUNCTION

The function of a room is a crucial factor when deciding on its color and finish. Will the room will be used throughout the day, or only in the evenings or at night? If you are painting a dining room, will it be used largely for formal evening entertaining, or is it likely to be filled throughout the day with family and children? If the first scenario applies, you can use darker colors regardless of whether there is much daylight, but for a family room, lighter colors with finishes that are easy to wash down and retouch would be more appropriate.

A bedroom should be painted in a shade that is restful and warming at night without seeming dull and oppressive in the morning light—the room is used at the two most psychologically sensitive periods of the day. Realistically, you may also have to spend more time in the room if you are sick, so you need colors that are relaxing without looking stale in daylight: mustard, cream and grayish greens are all best avoided.

Kitchens can take an enormous variety of paint effects, but because they tend to be warm and damp you should choose one with a finish that is durable, easily washed down, and that will neither obscure dirt nor appear so ethereal that a spot of cooking oil looks like a bullet hole in the wall.

With frequent changes of temperature and steamy atmospheres, bathrooms have similar requirements to those of kitchens. Take this

A wide variety of patterns, colors and decorating styles mix successfully in this spacious room, thanks largely to the neutral backdrop of stone-work and warm earth wall colors.
(BELOW)

into account when selecting your paint, but do not be afraid to experiment with effects such as colorwashing, sponging, marbling, stenciling, graining, lining or trompe l'oeil.

LIGHT

After function, light is the most important consideration when painting an interior. Most of us understand the principle that whereas some colors are "cold," others are "warm." Dark rooms with little direct sunlight generally need warming up, whereas those facing the sun can usually be painted in cooler tints with less risk of them appearing chilly and unwelcoming.

Sunlight is white and therefore without color; the colors of the spectrum only appear when they are separated through a prism. Nevertheless, evening light tends to have a yellower tinge, depending on the amount of dust in the atmosphere. Most artificial lighting, with the exception of natural-daylight bulbs, is golden yellow. In most circumstances, fluorescent lighting is visually detrimental to both color and atmosphere, and will alter your perception of a room dramatically. In general, pale colors tend to be the safest choices for walls and stand up under most lighting conditions. If, however, you intend to filter the natural daylight using blinds, shutters or heavy curtains and will rely on artificial lighting, a deeper color may be appropriate.

When choosing colors, find out how they look both in daylight and at night. Paint an area at least 2ft (60cm) square either directly onto the wall or on a piece of board and observe how it looks under all lighting conditions typical of the room. Manufacturer's color cards only tell you what the color itself looks like, not how it will appear in your room.

Vivid carmine-red makes a narrow stairway look warm and inviting, bouncing light off the walls and casting a rosy glow on the ceiling.
(RIGHT)

ROOM SHAPES

Soft green walls and a warm, creamy-white ceiling enhance the height of this living room. The lively gold and eau-de-Nil patterns of the dado panels create a transition between the light tones of the upper half of the room and the dark wood and wicker furniture.

(BELOW)

TALL ROOMS

Tall rooms are usually found in older properties such as the town houses and villas of the late Georgian, Victorian, and Edwardian periods. Unless these have been altered substantially, their proportions will generally be elegantly divided with ridged moldings or cornicing around the edge of the ceiling, a picture rail about 2ft (60cm) below, a chair rail or dado about 3ft (90cm) above the floor, and a relatively deep baseboard at the bottom of the walls. All these features once had a practical purpose, but they can also be manipulated if you wish to adjust the proportions of a room. To accentuate the height of a tall room, paint the area above the picture rail the same color as the wall below. To lower a tall room, carry the color of the ceiling down as far as the picture rail.

If your walls have no dividing features and you wish to lower the height of the room, paint the ceiling in a slightly darker shade than the walls or use a shading technique (see pages 84-5) to produce the desired effect.

LOW ROOMS

Unless you wish to stress the low nature of the space, paint the ceiling and walls of a low room in light colors. To add height to a low room, paint the ceiling in a lighter color than the walls, and the area above the picture rail in the same color as the wall below. Shading—in this case gradually darkening the wall color as it moves towards the floor—will make the room appear to grow lighter as the eye is drawn upward, giving a feeling of height.

NARROW ROOMS

Unless you enjoy the narrowness of a room, detract from the shape by using pale or bright color on the walls and ceiling. Dark walls combined with a pale ceiling will give the impression of a corridor.

WIDE ROOMS

Few people would deliberately lessen the width of a spacious area, but this can be achieved by painting two facing walls in a deeper tone of the color used on the other

two walls. Darkening alcoves or recesses on facing walls or finishing one or more walls in a contrasting color will also help to achieve this effect. Dark colors with a degree of weight, such as deep green or terracotta, will always "bring in" a room, demonstrating the principle that darkness visually closes in space.

IRREGULAR ROOMS

If you have a room that widens at one end, has one or more walls which slope inward to the ceiling, walls which are vertical but meet at awkward angles, or any combination of these, it is generally best to paint it in a uniform color or finish that will allow the unusual shape to speak for itself. L-shaped rooms have the advantage of a hidden annex which is only discovered as you walk through the room. The color and texture of the first part of the room can either be continued around the corner or you can

try a contrasting finish. The leg of an "L" lends itself particularly well to trompe l'oeil effects (see page 119), providing an aperture into a further, illusory space, such as a garden, an arbor, or a false alcove.

Although attics and other irregular-shaped rooms can be enhanced by a variety of different effects, it is wise to avoid overcomplicated patterning, such as marbling.

DARK ROOMS

If a room is naturally dark—whether it has very small windows or is permanently overshadowed—there is no point in fighting this tendency. Paint cannot provide light, only reflect it. Try painting the room in a warm, glowing color and illuminate it with bright or cosy lighting, or decorate it in paler tones and use natural-daylight bulbs. The darkest rooms tend to be attics, bathrooms and basements, so let your decision be ruled by how the space is to be used.

A dark, oppressive atmosphere has been avoided in this low-ceilinged attic room by painting the walls white and the heavy wooden beams a soft shade of duck-egg blue.
(ABOVE)

COLOR

Warm terracottas, greens and ochres and stylized black and gray trompe l'oeil designs have been used to evoke a hallway in ancient Pompeii.
(BELOW AND RIGHT)

Until two centuries ago, the colors and types of paint available had altered little for two thousand years. Even so, the incredible array of paint colors which we now take for granted are derived from around sixteen of the original pigments used in interior and exterior decoration. These "natural" colors have been rediscovered periodically by different designers and cultures to revitalize the whole concept of decorative painting.

Throughout history the use of color has been dictated by three factors: appearance, durability, and cost. The most coveted colors were those that looked brightest, lasted longest, and were the rarest and therefore highest in price. Those who could afford expensive colors used them as a means of gaining or maintaining prestige.

FRESCO COLORS

From ancient times it has been recognized that certain color pigments are suitable only for inks and fabrics. For example,

Tyrian purple, a color associated with the Caesars, was a fabric dye and could not be used on walls. Consequently, the paint pigments which could be used on plaster and wood were the colors that had the greatest influence on interior design. Many of these pigments were fresco colors—ground pigments which could be mixed with lime and either brushed into wet plaster (plaster which was touch dry) or applied to it *secco*, that is when it was properly dry.

The vibrant ultramarine-blue of the Italian Renaissance is combined with older fresco earth colors in patterns derived from ancient Greek and Roman art. These early fresco pigments formed the base from which the entire palette of modern-day paint colors has evolved.
(ABOVE)

ITALIAN RENAISSANCE COLORS

The Italian Renaissance saw a huge expansion in the variety of pigments used. Varying amounts of black or white were added to individual colors to obtain a whole range of tints and tones. The earth colors—raw and burnt sienna and raw and burnt umber—were by far the most widely used, because they were cheap and could often be dug locally. The pigments known and used during the period of the Italian Renaissance formed the basis of all decorative paint colors right up until the late eighteenth century.

EIGHTEENTH-CENTURY COLORS

Traditionally, the exteriors of eighteenth-century cottages and street dwellings were limewashed, while the interior walls were coated with distemper. This was the cheapest paint in use during the eighteenth century and was often known as "size color." Manufactured from ground chalk (whiting) mixed with glue size made from animal bones, it was usually tinted with a pigment, typically one of the earth colors such as yellow ochre or red oxide. However, more basic additions were not uncommon; for example, ox blood produced a rusty pink.

Although rarely used as a wall color during the eighteenth century, a golden yellow such as Soane's yellow (see pages 30–1) is a superb modern-day foil for the off-whites, soft stone grays, woodwork and furnishings of the period.
(BELOW)

As well as being cheap and easily tinted, distemper was also straightforward and quick to apply. On the other hand it was neither washable nor durable, as it is easy to rub off the walls. Today this chalk-and-size mix is often known as "soft distemper," to distinguish it from later varieties. (A recipe is given on page 210.)

While the wealthy owners of town and country houses often used distemper on their ceilings, they preferred to decorate walls and woodwork with oil-based paint, mixing the pigment with white or red lead and linseed oil. Ceilings remained off-white throughout the eighteenth century, and it was the way in which colors were used on walls which underwent the most radical changes during this period.

In the early Georgian period (c.1714–50) the walls of the most affluent houses were wood-paneled from ceiling to floor. These walls, including both baseboards and cornices, were typically painted with oil-based paint, either in cream or a mid-brown color called wainscot. Doors, baseboards, and shutters, although not usually the cornices, were sometimes painted in a darker tone such as walnut brown or chocolate, with the occasional baseboard painted in black. Woodgraining was also extremely popular, and wooden paneling was often painted to imitate different timbers such as oak, cedar, and walnut.

All this changed in about the middle of the century. The mid-Georgian period (c.1750–1800) witnessed a rapid lightening of interiors, largely because starting around 1740 the area covered by wood paneling or wainscoting was being steadily reduced and replaced by plaster. Chairs were traditionally placed around the walls when not in use, so a protective wooden dado rail was retained about 3ft (90cm) from the floor. Wood paneling was still commonly found below this level until the end of the century. The new plasterwork was

frequently painted in white, although it was always the white of whole milk rather than the brilliant whites available today. This was because the linseed oil into which the white lead was mixed yellowed rapidly. Yellow or brown earths were often added to the white to produce a "stone color," and occasionally blues or black were used to offset the yellowing.

Whereas white and stone paints were relatively inexpensive, new and costlier colors such as blossom, straw, orange, and lemon also appeared, along with darker shades such as olive, pea, and sky blue. The most expensive colors of all were the deep greens, based on verdigris, and

smalt, a direct descendant of Egyptian blue, consisting of powdered cobalt-blue glass and consequently used in only the wealthiest of households.

The late Georgian or Regency period (c.1801–37) witnessed the disappearance of wood paneling below the dado rail and the return of some of the strong, undiluted pigments used by the Greeks and Romans. Red and terracotta were very popular colors for dining areas and, rather surprisingly, as a background to pictures. Picture-gallery red provided an effective foil to the gilded frames of oil paintings, while libraries were often painted in crimson; a stone color was now most likely to be used in halls and stairways.

A pale blue recalling the color of Wedgwood ceramics, set against off-white woodwork, evokes the atmosphere of the Georgian era through its cool grace.
(ABOVE)

*Soft golden-ochre walls, a checkered floor and
minimal furnishings epitomize the spare grace of
the Adams style of the late eighteenth and early
nineteenth centuries.*

(ABOVE)

Green was by far the most dominant
color of the era. It appeared not only in
dining rooms, drawing rooms, stairways,
around windows, and on shutters and front
doors, but was also used outside on garden
furniture, fences and gates. Middle-class
households strove to link the interiors of
their homes with their gardens, choosing
greens that would harmonize with the trees
and shrubs, with additional colors to match
the flowers. During this period color
choices became influenced by the aspect of
a room: dark rooms were warmed with red,
lilac, buff or salmon, while those facing
the sun were cooled with shades of blue
and green.

During the eighteenth century the brickwork of houses was frequently faced with
stucco, a mixture of sand, cement and lime
applied wet over the brick. Stucco both
protected and made it possible to paint a
building, usually in imitation of more
expensive stone. The stone color most frequently applied to stucco could be anything
from sandy to blue-gray in tone, with window frames often painted in a coordinating
stone color. Doors were usually colored in
Spanish brown—a very deep reddish brown
similar to burnt sienna with black added—
or olive brown, an olive green with red and
black added. Towards the close of the eighteenth century window frames and glazing
bars were painted in similar dark colors,
giving windows the appearance of rectan-
gular voids in a façade.

Ironwork, such as gates and railings, was
often painted lead color or stone, but a particular favorite was invisible green, a green
so dark as to appear nearly black when
placed against a white surface. The most
wealthy households—or those with aspira-
tions to wealth—occasionally painted their
ironwork in dazzling smalt blue, the glass
grains giving the metal an iridescent
quality, which cost at least four times as
much as most other colors.

VICTORIAN COLORS

There is still a tendency to associate the use of dark colors with the Victorians, but this is partly erroneous. Most Victorian paint colors were similar to those of the later eighteenth century or the strong and vibrant tones of the Regency period. The heaviness of the stereotypical nineteenth-century interior was more often the result of shutting out light with heavy layers of curtaining, the use of oil and gas lamps, and the penchant for large, dark-toned furniture. The effect was accentuated by the new and immensely popular mauve and purple dyes used in fabrics and wallpapers. The overriding feature of the Victorian era was the increasing complexity of the color schemes, with great care taken to balance light and shade.

During the 1840s lilac and salmon paints were very fashionable, with paler tints of these and other strong colors, such as crimson, terracotta, picture-gallery red and warm greens making frequent appearances in dining rooms. Sage green and Hunter green came to dominate bedrooms and libraries, but it is interesting to note that although paint technology during the 1820s and '30s made blues and yellows far less costly than before, these colors appeared only rarely in Victorian houses.

In great contrast to eighteenth-century fashion, the Victorians delighted in picking out the moldings on ceilings, cornices and architraves in contrasting and often quite vivid colors. The wall below the dado rail was frequently decorated with embossed paper, typically in a deep Hunter green or purple-brown, or grained to imitate wood such as mahogany. This decoration was intended to create a transition between the dark patterned carpet and the lighter

Victorian-style black-painted ironwork, picture-gallery red walls and an off-white ceiling give this functional room a feeling of spaciousness and warmth.
(ABOVE)

walls. The moldings at the top of the wall were then picked out in a color lighter than the dado but stronger and richer than the walls themselves.

Creamy off-white distemper was frequently used on Victorian ceilings, but by the 1850s richly colored ceilings had become common even in modest households. A typical drawing-room color scheme might consist of a mahogany wood-grained door, Hunter-green embossed dado panel, grained or purple-brown dado rail, lilac walls, and a light blue-green, cream or pale salmon ceiling. The moldings around the ceiling, and roses around light fittings, might be picked out in an alternating mixture of terracotta, lilac, cream, blue-green and salmon.

The advent of electric lighting and the Queen Anne revival of the 1890s brought in the practice of painting woodwork white. Electricity did not possess the softness of gas and oil lamps, and its harsh light revealed fading and discoloring, as well as altering the appearance of many colors which had previously been enhanced by the yellowness of the older lighting.

Green was the most popular exterior paint color of the era. Both woodwork and metalwork were typically painted in various shades of Hunter green, or, alternatively, in bronze-green, which gave metalwork the appearance of weathered bronze. Purple-brown was sometimes used on window frames and doors, along with crimson, combined with black door furniture. As in the eighteenth century, brick walls were almost never painted, but stucco walls were generally colored in dark or light stone, yellow ochre, or buff.

Lilacs and mauves were enduringly popular throughout the Victorian era. With the advent of electric lighting in the 1890s, woodwork was often brightened with white paint.

(LEFT)

EDWARDIAN COLORS

The opening years of the twentieth century saw a revolution in paint technology which surpassed every development of the previous two hundred years. As in most new centuries, the first decade was largely a cultural continuation of the century before. Edwardian style was less cluttered than that of the Victorians but, in huge contrast to the Art Deco style which would follow the First World War, it was backward looking in its old-fashioned elegance. However, the Scandinavian-influenced white baseboard and woodwork and light walls of the Queen Anne revival left a lasting legacy. These colors rapidly became popular in middle-class suburban homes and have remained almost universally the taste of the public throughout the twentieth century. Art Deco style simply reinforced this preference.

Greens, immensely popular with the Victorians, were still prevalent in more pastel shades, following the Adams style of the 1890s. However, although Adam green is possibly the color we associate most strongly with this period, cool and strong shades of blue also came back into favor. The typical interior of an affluent Edwardian household might be painted with a white ceiling, eau-de-Nil, primrose or azure walls and a white dado rail, baseboard and door frame. The door might be white, or, alternatively, a deep Indian or Venetian red, or possibly grained in imitation of oak or

The light colors and forms of late eighteenth-century Scandinavian schemes were widely imitated in the Edwardian period in reaction against some of the darker late-Victorian interiors.
(BELOW)

wallpaper were sometimes varnished, allowing them to be wiped down. To this end, washable distempers appeared from the 1870s. Cheaper than oil paints and more durable than their old size-based forebears, these were also credited with disinfecting properties.

Although lead continued to be used widely in paint until the 1950s, many colors were gradually being produced in less toxic forms. New developments in chemical dyes made colors brighter and stronger than ever before, as well as providing a greater degree of consistency. During the eighteenth and nineteenth centuries there was rarely any consistency between different manufacturer's versions of the same color. By the early years of the twentieth century, however, paint manufacture had become increasingly reliable and the first attempt to standardize paint names was made in 1906. This was followed by the production of tint charts, demonstrating the effects of varying proportions of white on the colors available, and these innovations helped to establish a standard color range by 1930.

Although Art Deco dominated the style of public buildings such as movie theaters and restaurants through the inter-war years, its influence on domestic decor was limited to those with high incomes. The interior decoration of modest suburban and terraced houses in the 1920s and '30s was dominated by soft beiges and browns: dark brown was common on woodwork, and off-white or white distemper on unpapered ceilings.

Edwardian exterior decoration resembled that of the Victorian era. Gloss greens such as Hunter and deep bronze-green were popular for doors; black or dark Hunter green or bronze-green for railings and other ironwork. The chief innovation was the return to painting window frames and glazing bars white, although masonry continued to be painted cream, taupe, or stone.

The Victorian practice of painting softwood to resemble costlier hardwood continued well into the twentieth century, but furniture gained a new freshness now that it was set against the lighter walls of Edwardian interiors.

(ABOVE)

mahogany. Strong colors like azure, dark blue, royal blue, and brilliant green were commonly used, especially in gloss form, on woodwork such as baseboards and paneling.

The introduction of enamel in paint meant that gloss finishes and flat oil were now easier to apply. The Edwardians found that light colors looked best in an eggshell finish, a particular advantage as hygiene was an Edwardian obsession and such finishes were easy to clean. The preoccupation with cleanliness meant that oil-based paint and

ART DECO COLORS

Considered the height of the avant-garde, this style of decoration was largely the preserve of high income groups, but its influence was enormous. In total contrast to the elegant retrospection of Edwardian times, Art Deco was a celebration of strong color, clean line and a paring down of decoration. Moldings, dado rails, and cornices all vanished from the Art Deco room and, initially at least, the new paints in their strong colors were given free rein.

Gloss paints were used on walls as well as eggshell finishes, and could be anything from golden yellow, signal red, peacock or azure blue to black. Walls were frequently picked out with stencil designs. A typical Art Deco room might have had a white or yellow ceiling and light battleship-gray walls, with signal-red doors and yellow door frames, baseboard and window frame, and green and yellow wall stencils.

Bedroom colors were often softer, with shades of lilac, cool turquoise, ice blue and green. White, too, dominated the Art Deco age. Interiors were sometimes painted in a dozen different tints of white, from cream and brilliant bleached whites to pinky or greeny white, matched with white furniture, ornaments and fabric.

Lining, or striping, was also a major feature of Art Deco style, with geometric patterns taking the place of moldings and cornices, generally in a contrasting color to the main areas but sometimes in a darker or lighter tint or tone of the dominant color. The effect was often carried through to coordinating patterns stenciled onto furniture. Stenciling also appeared in frieze motifs, as accents on the corners of doors or walls, or as a dominant feature in its own right. These stencils were consciously modernist in appearance, with the sleek, fluid forms and sudden angles seen in the poster designs of Ernest Dryden and Erté, and the sculpture of Hagenauer and Marcel Bourraine.

Marbling was an important element of the Art Deco interior, particularly in the less important areas of commercial buildings such as movie theaters and hotels, where to use the real stone would be too costly. The technique also appeared in enclosed areas such as bathrooms, where Belgian black or Thessalian green were highly favored.

Architecture was notable for its brightness. Exterior walls were usually white—a brilliant, bleached tone painted onto a very smooth surface. Geometric patterns were sometimes picked out in bold, contrasting hues, while the new metal window frames were painted white or bright green, ice blue, dark blue, eau-de-Nil, black or signal red.

Clean, geometric patterns, strong painted backgrounds and a paring down of decorative detail gave Art Deco interiors an understated elegance. (BELOW)

COLOR SCHEMES

Neutral silvery-gray walls give this room a feeling of space. The cool color enhances the warmth of the gold, burgundy and indigo of the furnishings.
(BELOW)

Just as there is no such thing as an ugly room, neither is there an ugly color, but it is possible to end up with unfortunate color partnerships. Before decorating a room or anything else, it is worth taking the time to find out how colors behave in combination with each other. This will help you to avoid some of the common pitfalls that can occur when decorating with different hues, allowing you to derive the greatest pleasure from their variety.

NEUTRALS AND NATURALS

A neutral color is a tint or tone that will sit comfortably alongside any other color. Although made up of a number of colors, gray is probably the color most often associated with neutrality because visually it falls halfway between black and white, neither of which is strictly a color at all. It may be warm or cool, depending on the degree of blue or yellow it contains. Grays are so versatile and subtle that an entire decor may be built up around them, providing, in effect, the paint equivalent of a monotone photograph.

Most colors can play a neutral role if they are used as a passive background to other colors. For instance, one might not think of so powerful a color as scarlet-red being a neutral, but if an entire room is painted in it then any objects of a different color will automatically become the focus of attention. However, it would be fair to say that neutral colors are more frequently understood to be "natural" shades such as pale stone, soft earth colors, gray-greens and dusty blues.

The natural colors of the stone floor and wooden furniture combine well with the light earth color of the plaster in this rustic interior. The furnishings have been carefully chosen to complement their surroundings.
(ABOVE)

This attractive scheme brings together the neutral buff tones of stone, plaster, canvas and linen.
(LEFT)

REDS AND PINKS

After yellow (see pages 30-1), red is the most visually dominating color. Paint manufacturers refer to this characteristic as "chroma," or the brightness of a color in relation to its pigment density. Red is usually thought of as a warm color, as it appears to move towards us. Its primal associations with fire and blood mean that red is often seen as both grand and aggressive; in the Middle Ages, only the more important members of society were allowed to wear red cloth.

Red is a color of great "weight," as well as brightness. In a children's playroom, signal red or poppy red on walls or furniture can give a sense of vibrancy and excitement, whereas deeper reds like crimson, picture-gallery red or cadmium scarlet can look sumptuous in a dining room. Flat red paint evokes the luxury of velvet and is appropriate for formal spaces such as studies, boardrooms, and restaurants. Gloss red—red is one of the small number of colors which work well in gloss on a wall—can look striking in a dining room if used with conviction.

Warm pink, seen in a cool light, has been balanced against a warm light blue of equal intensity. Pink can appear rather chilly in a dark room, and works best where it has a strong color to support it.
(ABOVE RIGHT)

Fiery red, ragrolled over a warm yellow, is most intense in color when the light is indirect. The dark woodwork would appear dull and oppressive against a softer-colored wall.
(RIGHT)

On an exterior, red can bestow an air of sophistication or dismal banality. Few things could be less successful than an attempt to give a badly designed block of apartments an air of effervescence by painting the doors in geranium red: everything else will look even shabbier in contrast, and the sense of anonymity and regimentation will be increased. On the other hand, a burgundy-red gloss door on an Edwardian street house, or Venetian-red glazing bars outlined with broken white on a 1930s suburban house, can look superb.

In contrast, pink has a reputation for softness. Ranging from deep, vivid shades to almost white, it can be warm or cool. A room decorated entirely in pink may turn out looking like an overblown flower garden or an explosion in a strawberry ice-cream factory, but if used judiciously, pink

can be a valuable decorating color. For instance, dusty or dusky pinks (pinks containing yellow or grays and blues respectively) are versatile and can act as good coordinating shades among reds, yellows, blues and browns. They will also reflect warmly in a room with a predominantly yellow tone or lighting, and coolly amid blues in a more shaded situation.

Traditionally, pink has been used as a tint for the distemper and colorwash used both inside and on the exteriors of cottages, small street houses, and farm buildings. It was also used as an alternative to white on the exteriors of Art Deco houses.

Deep raspberry pink becomes "bluer" against red furniture. A more violet pink would have made the crimson seem "off-hue" or too brown.

(RIGHT)

ORANGES AND YELLOWS

Orange is the meeting point of the spectrum's two brightest colors, red and yellow, but it is also less strident, possessing neither the weight of red nor the airiness of yellow. As a result, it can provide a lovely tawny link between other tones. Many woodgraining tints and tones are variants of orange, as are numerous color-washes and shades of marble. The two great earth colors, yellow ochre and burnt sienna, blend to a tone of orange that is almost always warm and clean in appearance and rarely heavy or dull.

Yellow is the brightest color of the spectrum. With its intense chroma, yellow can be both warm and cold. Warm yellows, on the red side of the spectrum, reflect light to give off a warm glow. Their drawback is that only a limited range of colors can be used with them in most domestic interiors. This is because many pastels and "secondary colors" (colors mixed from any two primaries) tend to look dull beside them. Only the primaries red and blue, and the strong secondary, purple, can stand up to yellow *en masse*. However, pale yellow can be very successful if it is used as a foil to stronger colors which might otherwise smother their background.

Yellow is ideal for use in a playroom or bathroom, or to warm up a shaded bedroom. Soane's yellow, the color used by Sir John Soane in his Small Drawing Room at Lincoln's Inn Fields, London, was a close relation of Turner's yellow. Although not

The intense yellow of this hallway is balanced by the strong primary hues of the adjoining rooms.
(LEFT)

A yellow ochre on an undulating wall, with a heavier terra-verte gray-green below, makes a perfect backdrop for chunky antique woodwork.
(BELOW RIGHT)

widely used, this unusual color adorned the more formal, classical interiors of late eighteenth- and early nineteenth-century town and country houses.

One difficulty when using yellow lies in its capacity to reflect any other dominant color present in the light source. A warm yellow room overlooking a large tree or lawn may pick up the green tones, turning the color rather "acid." Filtering the daylight using white or cream curtains, or applying a very thin coat of white-tinted matte varnish over the yellow, will lessen this effect.

Lemon yellow can brighten the dingiest of corners. Ragged brushwork blends the color into the white ceiling for a soft finish.
(ABOVE LEFT)

A vibrant deep orange gives a great sense of warmth without too much weight.
(ABOVE)

GREENS

Green has long been one of the most popular interior and exterior decorating colors. Darker greens can look either cool or warm, but all tend to have a formal look which is best complemented by woodwork painted in pale or deep-toned colors. Unlike yellow, dark green tends to absorb colored light, therefore its appearance alters little

A strong green gives structure to a white room which might otherwise become an airy void. Cool colors, such as the lilac and blue of the furnishings, need support to prevent them from being "bleached out" by white.
(ABOVE)

whatever the lighting conditions. Most objects stand out well against a background of dark greens, and paint with a flat finish looks particularly handsome in formal rooms, hallways, and bedrooms. In bathrooms, however, it may give a somewhat municipal impression. High-gloss dark green—like gloss red—can look positively regal on walls, particularly in a dining room. Green invariably works well as an exterior color on wood or ironwork, largely because it fits in with any natural surrounding greenery.

Light greens have very different properties when compared to darker shades. Because they are pale they can reflect large

quantities of light, making other colors appear far more dominating than they really are. Clean tints give a great sense of space and tranquility, whereas murkier tones used in the wrong place can be oppressive.

Most light greens look best when applied in eggshell or flat finishes, as in a gloss finish they have a tendency to appear cold, governmental, and even tawdry. It is best to avoid using yellowish light greens in dimly lit areas, as they can take on the sickly appearance of an unhealthy plant. However, used in clear light and juxtaposed against white, yellowish greens can be highly effective. Light greens are particularly versatile colors for use in lining, spattering, and stenciling techniques.

Green shadows make a room look cool rather than cold. Here, a duck-egg green wall acquires a soft apple-green shadow where it is shielded from the light.
(ABOVE)

The natural hues of wood, cloth and leather appear rich against a backdrop of strong forest green. A colder, paler wall color would make them seem drab, while a darker shade would absorb too much light.
(LEFT)

BLUES

Blue has long been one of the most valued and expensive of pigments. In the color spectrum, blue is a long-wavelength color, which means that it appears to recede. For this reason, and because it is the hue of a cloudless sunlit sky, the color is frequently associated with ideas of infinity and spirituality. Dark blue, the shade of the midnight sky, is synonymous with authority and is considered by Buddhists to be a holy color.

In its paler tints, blue can be airy, cool, or warm. On the green or yellow side of the spectrum, it gives a sensation of brilliance or vast depth, but it can sometimes be too dominant in an interior because of its powerful chroma, making the yellower earth colors appear grubby and the reds too harsh. Pale blues on the red and lilac side of

Cobalt blues are bright and warm rather than chilly, and complement raw- and burnt-umber browns.
(RIGHT)

Turquoise blue can be oppressively heavy over large areas, but has a lightening effect when used to pick out details such as door panels and window frames.
(BELOW)

Rich ultramarine-blue (often dubbed "royal blue") accented by burnt sienna, a powerful earth red, gives this tiny washroom a stylish finish.
(RIGHT)

This open stairway has been decorated with blues from the red side of the spectrum. The strong ultramarine woodwork gives the space a sense of structure, while a "frosty" pale blue frames the pale carmine-pink window.
(FAR RIGHT)

the spectrum are usually cold, but they harmonize more readily with other colors because their coolness makes them appear to recede.

Used externally, lighter blues can appear rather tacky if they are too "sweet" in tone, so it is often best to stick to darker shades. Dark blues, especially those on the redder side of the spectrum, possess quite different qualities.

There is a great difference between a dark blue and a bright blue; Oxford blue, for example, is both dark and bright, whereas midnight blue is dark and deep. Oxford blue looks superb against off-whites, deep red-browns and, in the right places, red-yellows. Midnight blues are powerful in flat, eggshell or gloss and look particularly elegant in formal rooms and on doors.

PURPLES

Purple was a favorite color in the ancient world. It was the color of the raiments of the emperors of Rome, and a costly purple fabric dye made from shellfish was exported all over the Middle East and Mediterranean. The purple used on walls was less precious, and was made by mixing red and blue pigments. In the cooler light of northern Europe, however, purple did not become a popular decorating color until the middle of the nineteenth century. Like dark blue, it works well with off-whites and deep reds, as well as blue-greens. In recent years, the color has become associated with the psychedelic subcultures of the 1960s and is now more often used as a fabric color than for interior decoration.

Lilac and mauve were widely used in the mid-nineteenth century after the discovery of a stable pigment for these tints (see page 21). Although generally better suited to interiors than exteriors, these shades can be used almost anywhere in their lighter tones. Certain color combinations should be avoided: both lilacs and mauves can appear too "sweet" when juxtaposed with mustard yellow, the latter looking very grubby by comparison. However, both shades work superbly with silver-grays, dusty blues, soft greens, deep sienna reds and deep yellows.

Few colors are richer in conjunction with gold than purple, and very few can support its lustre with more panache. Conversely, the "prettier" purple tones of the 1960s give a much lighter look.
(BELOW)

Various lilac tones brushed on with a broken-color technique give these dining-room walls depth and variety, and form the perfect backdrop for brightly colored furnishings and accessories.
(LEFT)

Balancing beautifully with the clean, sandy yellows of the woodwork, two closely related mauve tones have been applied with a criss-cross brush technique that prevents the colors from looking "flat."
(BELOW)

BROWNS AND BLACKS

Brown encompasses the whole range of earth colors from yellows to reds, as well as including the siennas and umbers, and overlapping into olive greens and purple-reds. Perhaps the most versatile of all decorating colors, the browns rarely clash with each other and they will complement most other tints and tones.

Mustard, however, which is as close to the yellows as it is to the browns, sits unhappily with light blues and mauves, and darker browns lack vigor when used against light greens (the walls and linoleum of old municipal buildings are a monument to this), but generally there is nothing insipid in the splendid versatility of these colors.

Strictly speaking, black is not a color at all, being the opposite of all light, that is, absolute darkness. However, in pigment form blacks can be very varied. Lampblack

is probably the nearest approximation to pure, colorless dark. Bone black (from charred bone) has a brownish tone, while vine black has a bluish undertone.

Used externally, blacks in gloss form have traditionally been applied to doors and weatherboarding. Inside, black is rarely used over large areas unless an extreme contrast is required, for example in a flat black room with white fabric, furniture and carpet, or a gloss black bathroom with white fixtures. If used with confidence, black can look superb both on woodwork such as furniture, floors and doors, and on walls.

Black walls with a brown undertone are elegant without being hard or oppressive. Other colors, including the black of the picture frames, appear fresh against them.
(BELOW)

Black and brown walls and woodwork need to be offset by paler or contrasting floors or furnishings to prevent them becoming too dull and heavy.
(ABOVE)

Earth browns harmonize well with greens. Here, shades of reddish brown produce a mellow effect.
(ABOVE RIGHT)

Browns from the red-purple end of the spectrum mottled over a gray-beige base: cool rust colors can look formal, as here, or informal, depending on the colors and objects set against them.
(RIGHT)

JUXTAPOSING COLORS

Many of us tend to rely on our instincts when deciding whether or not a certain combination of colors is successful. These feelings are based not only on our personal preferences but also on the properties of light and on the pigments themselves—one color always affects how we see another. For instance, a pale blue may appear very ethereal and light, perhaps with a greenish tint, when contrasted with a dark brown, whereas it might seem quite heavy, even rather gray, beside an airy, pinkish white. The range of colors is so vast that it would be impossible to state categorically which colors do or do not work well together, but choices are easier to make if we understand the reasons why some color combinations are unsuccessful and know what measures can be taken to avoid this.

A color wheel showing the primary colors—red, blue and yellow—with their "secondaries" interspaced between them. Orange therefore appears between red and yellow, green between yellow and blue, and purple between blue and red. "Complementary" colors of equal intensity occur opposite each other across the wheel; for example, turquoise blue appears opposite tangerine.
(RIGHT)

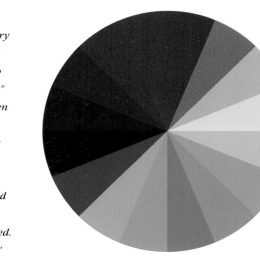

Most of us already know that there are three primary colors: red, blue and yellow. If we mix any two of these we produce what are termed the "secondary" colors; for example, red with blue makes purple, red with yellow makes orange, and yellow with blue makes green. If we then mix any two secondary colors we get a "tertiary" color; for example, purple with green makes olive green.

Adding white to a primary, secondary or tertiary color will produce a "tint," while adding black instead of white to any of them will produce a "shade." A "tone" is obtained when both black and white are added to a color; this term is also used to describe the visual intensity of one color in relation to another. Two colors of the same intensity are said to be of the same "tonal value:" emerald green and vermilion-red

may have the same intensity, although neither contain any white. Likewise, pink and sky blue both have the same intensity and both contain white. It is mismanagement of tone which results in problems.

DISCORDANT COLORS

Colors are what is termed "discordant" when the tones are wrong. If a lot of white is added to a naturally dark color like aubergine, so that it becomes a pale grayish pink, and then an equal amount of black is added to a pale color like apple green, the natural relationship between the two colors will have been reversed; they are now discordant. If they are used alongside each other in equal quantities each color will appear to smother the other; it is the visual equivalent of eating mustard and strawberry jam together.

A successful juxtaposition of primary and secondary colors. The colors are all of equal visual strength, and work in harmony to give this room a bright and vibrant appearance.

(ABOVE)

Blue-gray and acid yellow, two tints that are very difficult to use in conjunction, work together success- fully here because the yellow is "clean" enough to stand out from the wall. If the yellow was browner in tone, the two colors would become "discordant."
(RIGHT)

Apple green and scarlet red are near "complementaries" (opposites of equal intensity). Here, the addition of a strong blue prevents a visual tug-of-war between two powerful hues.
(CENTER)

Perfectly balanced complementary hues, with each color given equal weight, have been used across walls, doors and moldings to break the architectural monotony of a hallway.
(FAR RIGHT)

OFF-HUES

When blue and red are mixed together they produce purple. If an ultramarine blue is placed directly beside a violet purple, (which is much nearer red than blue) the two colors will throw each other "off-hue." They will appear to alter each other: the dark blue will look yellower and the violet rosier. It is preferable to find a link between two colors.

COMPLEMENTARY COLORS

A complementary color is the name given to a color on the opposite side of the spectrum to another of equal intensity. For example, turquoise is a complementary of tangerine; red violet is a comple- mentary of golden yellow; orange of azure; scarlet of viridian green. These are called

"complementaries" rather than opposites because, in theory, if you mix the pure pigments of any two complementaries they will cancel each other out, producing a grayish color. In practice, most commercial decorating paints contain a great deal of filler so if you mix two complementaries of these paints you will probably end up with something more like camouflage paint.

Complementary colors can be exciting. If you place two side by side you will get a "color buzz:" the colors will appear to over-lap slightly along a flickering gray line. This means that any color can be toned down, or "grayed," by the addition of a small amount of its complementary. For example, a little green added to an overpowering red will soften it and a touch of orange will warm a hard, chilly blue.

However, in the long run there is nothing to stop you using any combination of colors you like, so long as they please you; this information is intended only as a guide and offers the most likely explanations of what has happened if you end up with color mixes which do not succeed.

WHETHER YOU WANT TO DECORATE A TINY ENTRANCE HALL OR A SPACIOUS MASTER BEDROOM, DECIDING ON A DECORATIVE SCHEME IS NEVER EASY. THIS ROOM-BY-ROOM SURVEY OF SUCCESSFUL PAINT PROJECTS PROVIDES A WEALTH OF INSPIRATIONAL IDEAS.

inspiration

MOST DECORATING PROJECTS STEM from a single moment of inspiration, but deciding exactly what you want to do is often the most difficult part of the operation. Although having a variety of paint colors, textures and techniques to choose from offers wonderful opportunities, it can also be bewildering. The best way to find your creative bearings is to focus on the main use of the room you wish to decorate and see if that presents any limitations or opportunities to experiment; for example, painting a child's playroom will require a totally different approach than decorating a guest bedroom. Next, decide whether or not you intend to retain the existing furnishings. What will harmonize with their  *colors and textures and what will not? It is usually wise to avoid very complex schemes, as domestic surroundings tend to possess their own visual variety. In any case, you can easily embellish a painted surface later on if you find it too plain; the reverse scenario would be more problematic.*

With a little imagination, paint can transform any living space. An artificially lit, unremarkable hallway gains life and movement from an exuberant abstract design painted in blue and ochre.

HALLS AND STAIRWAYS

A harmonious marriage of natural and painted foliage and off-white color-washed plaster decorated with delicate scroll patterns brings this hallway to life.
(BELOW)

Halls and stairways are where most visitors gain their first and often strongest impressions of a house. Although people rarely linger in these places, it is well worth spending time and effort on them. They are often well-lit and free of clutter, so you can indulge in a riot of color, pattern, and texture without having to worry about the added complication of furnishings and other fixtures.

Cool blocks of well-balanced pastel tints
complement the light wood of this stairway and
landing. The lilac appears almost blue in the
shadows beyond, and gives a sense of focus
and destination.

(ABOVE)

The spare elegance of this stairway, bathed in
natural light, is balanced by the deep texture of
distressed, colorwashed walls (see pages 78–83).
The mellow gray tones avoid bleakness and
anchor the room's other strong features: the
marble table and stained wooden treads.

(LEFT)

LIVING ROOMS

An evenly applied, golden-ochre color-wash gives the richly textured furnishings in this tall room the glow of an Old Master painting. The pale ceiling is balanced by a high-level frieze.

(BELOW)

The living room is where most people spend the majority of their domestic time and as such it attracts the greatest amount of decorative attention; such rooms are usually the most spacious, well-lit and extensively furnished in the home. A successful paint scheme should create a harmonious environment which can be lived with happily and enjoyed for some years before you feel the need for a change.

Stippling on an ivory-colored glaze (see page 95) has created a restful, warm glow in this living room, offering a soft foil to the grisaille-patterned fabric frieze and pelmet, marbled mantel and off-white molded plasterwork.

(RIGHT)

The strong, textured color blocks of the pictures in this living room are balanced by the rough, vertical dragging, or strié, technique used on the walls (see pages 92–3), the fire screen's robust lined disc motifs, and the whitened ceiling.
(LEFT)

An elegant combination of lilac and light jade green complements the wooden table and flooring, and the gilt-framed mirror.
(LEFT)

An expansive living space is given a sense of drama by two bold "fresco" colors: a solid ultramarine and a dragged terracotta.
(BELOW)

STUDIES AND WORKROOMS

A beautiful balance of blue-gray and dusty-ochre eggshell washes is enhanced by the gloss stencils (see pages 98–101) which catch the light in this confined space. The ochre patterning of tarnished gilt stars picks up and mirrors the textures of the furnishings.
(BELOW)

Studies are visually "busy" rooms, filled with books, computers, work tables, and adjustable lighting. Colors need to be conducive to concentration: either vibrant and stimulating without being overpowering, or tranquil and offering clean light. If you intend to conduct business meetings at home, your study should convey the appropriate atmosphere. Workrooms, on the other hand, are essentially practical spaces: paint finishes need to be durable and generally neutral so as to allow objects to be viewed clearly against them, but without appearing dull, negative, or "energy sapping."

Off-white eggshell makes a clean backdrop for the checkered floor and the fretwork of light and shade created by wood, cloth, and gleaming metal.
(CENTER LEFT, ABOVE)

The broken geometry and strong colors of a linear wall design add interest to this study area, leading the eye alternately back and forth.
(CENTER LEFT, BELOW)

This is cool gray at its most elegant. Strong and versatile, the color does not overwhelm the diverse functional furnishings in this comfortable study. The "weight" of the furniture is balanced by the graceful dark gray Greek frieze and the crisp, earth-red lining (see pages 96–7).
(LEFT)

KITCHENS

Cobalt-blue eggshell on wood-paneled walls emphasizes the structure of this simple, farmhouse-style kitchen. The darker bluish-gray is a practical choice for the floor and a perfect foil for the brightness of the blue and white above.
(BELOW)

Although they are first and foremost practical spaces, kitchens nonetheless have enormous decorative potential. Style-wise, there are few limits as to how they can be painted, and stenciling, lining work, and painted furniture all work well in these locations. As they are rarely covered by carpets, rugs, or mats, kitchen floors offer good opportunities for painting and varnishing, or for laying colorfully painted tiles. However, you must bear in mind that painted surfaces in kitchens should ideally be durable and easy to wipe down, as these rooms are often subject to extremes of temperature, steam, and condensation.

The elegant furnishings and generous window of this tall room offered David Carter the perfect opportunity to create this regal treatment of dark indigo, cream, and gold. The frieze makes the ceiling look higher than it actually is, while the vertical lining design is another piece of visual trickery, accentuating the length of the walls. The overall scheme is effective due to the room's spectacular location as much as its function, and would work equally well in a dining room or living room.

(LEFT)

Kitchens are often eclectic, informal living spaces and offer great scope for experimenting with craft techniques. Here, a distressed ochre colorwash (see pages 78-83) applied over cream plaster acts as a backdrop for a kitchen dresser decorated with stencil designs (pages 98-101) and lining work (pages 96-7).

(ABOVE)

These rich colors give form to what would otherwise be a characterless and clinically functional space. The flat olive green ceiling complements the burgundy wall, as both colors are of similar intensity.

(LEFT)

These freehand swirl wall designs create an exuberant sense of movement, balancing the robust, chunky patterns on the cupboards.

(RIGHT)

DINING ROOMS

Formal or informal, dining rooms offer almost as much decorative scope as kitchens. They can look rustic or regal, quietly elegant, or comfortable and family-friendly, but you should bear in mind when and how you are going to use them—in the evening for entertaining or with the whole family throughout the day (or both)—as this will affect your choice of paint. Like kitchens, dining rooms are suitable locations for painted furniture and stencil designs, although the latter work best when they are quite formal in style.

(see pages 78–83).

A large dining room
with a decidedly
"antique" appearance,
achieved by stripping
the fixed woodwork
and distressing the
walls with two colored
glazes—yellow ochre
and blue-gray—over
a creamy-white base
(see pages 78–83).
The distressing is
deliberately patchy,
resembling layers of
colored plaster which
have peeled away over
many years.
(LEFT)

This spacious dining area consists of two rooms unified by a vertical striping pattern (see pages 96–7). The stripes are of equal width, but as those in the foreground appear to broaden, they give the room an illusory sense of height and space.

(ABOVE)

The height of this small, narrow room has been exaggerated by extending the white ceiling down to picture-rail level and applying a crisp gold-leaf frieze to draw the eye upwards. The rich color scheme of gold, vibrant green, blue, earth reds and browns has an Ancient Egyptian theme, and creates a sumptuous atmosphere in what would otherwise be an unremarkable space.

(RIGHT)

Distressed gray-pink has a velvety softness that balances the sharp, spare furniture but is subtle enough not to smother the cool colors of the rest of this room.

(ABOVE)

This dining-room table and bench have been vigorously distressed in those areas where wear and tear would naturally occur, creating a convincing and attractive look of age.

(LEFT)

BEDROOMS

Rich tones of purple, burgundy, and gold create a luxurious feel in this bedroom, making it seem cozy rather than confined. The pale ceiling prevents the dark colors from dominating or making the room appear gloomy.
(BELOW)

Bedrooms are often the trickiest rooms to decorate. They are intimate, private spaces, our personal havens from the outside world. They are also the places we retreat to when we are sick. Ideally they should be at once relaxing and gently stimulating; this may sound like a tall order, but some bright colors, such as strong blues, can be both. However, bear in mind that a vivid scarlet or dazzling yellow can look wonderful when you are falling into bed after a party, but may appear harsh when you wake up in the morning with a headache.

The golden ochre used to decorate the walls of this Arabian-style bedroom casts a warm and inviting glow. The white-painted frame of the doorway accentuates its elegant curves.
(ABOVE)

A successful marriage of blue-gray and yellow-taupe, traditionally an awkward color combination. The plain white bed coverings enhance the simplicity of the scheme and act as a neutral buffer between the other two colors.
(RIGHT)

Deep cherry pink, a traditional color for cottage interiors, gives this bedroom great warmth. Using the same shade of paint throughout the room distracts from the fact that the renovated ceiling is unusually flat in comparison with the rippling surface of the walls.
(RIGHT)

An arch effect painted onto these undulating cottage walls prevents an enclosed, box-like atmosphere. The white areas give a feeling of height; the green a cosy, cocooning effect.
(BELOW)

Freehand painted designs on a colorwashed wall (see pages 78–83) give this room a look of gracefully faded grandeur. The result is restful but not dull, thanks to the design's sense of movement.
(BELOW RIGHT)

A lively ultramarine applied over a white base can be dramatic or soothing,
depending on lighting and on mood. The white curtaining "cleans" the
incoming light and prevents any yellow or green tones from the garden outside
from intruding and causing the blue to appear too dark, heavy, and harsh.

(ABOVE)

CHILDREN'S ROOMS

This seaside design has a delightful sense of movement, created by the muted but lively coloring and the pale blue paneling following the outlines of the room.
(BELOW)

Children's rooms should reflect the interests and tastes of the children who use them. They should not be so "preciously" decorated that they are too elegant to play in, and if the children are very young, they should not feature colors or shapes that might frighten them at night. Accept that children almost always like bright hues, and may enjoy color combinations which set adult teeth on edge.

Children's rooms offer the chance to enjoy experimenting with random images and streaks or patches of color which would rarely work elsewhere.
(LEFT)

Strong light blues and greens combine in striping, stippling, stenciling, and freehand painting to give a cleverly planned impression of spontaneity.
(CENTER)

The pale painted tree with its cross-like structure holds this fantasy design together and lends support to the surrounding vivid colors. The unusual cupboard seems to blend almost magically into the painted background.
(ABOVE)

BATHROOMS

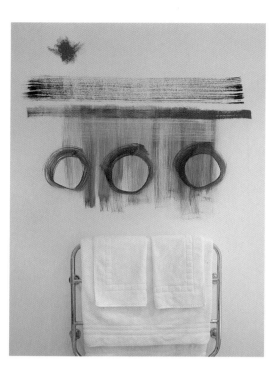

*A pale silvery-gray
wall color illuminates
this small bathroom,
and sets off the crisp
white of the bath and
warmer colors of the
distressed cupboards
and towel rail.*

(BELOW)

An immense range of paint effects, from marbling and ragging to stenciling and trompe l'oeil, can be used in bathrooms to create a look that is as charming, opulent, or exuberantly regal as you choose. Although certain constraints often occur in bathrooms, such as lack of space, limited light, and the need for surfaces to be both durable and steam resistant, an imaginative approach ensures that such apparent limitations can be used to your advantage.

Enlivening a plain white wall, this abstract design of freehand circles and rough brushstrokes in red, blue, and black has been carefully executed, but appears highly spontaneous.
(LEFT CENTER, ABOVE)

A distressed colorwash of warm gray and ochre makes a beautiful foil for polished metal, and visually "opens up" this confined space. The green marbling effect (see pages 108–11) below the baseboard balances the marble shelf.
(LEFT CENTER, BELOW)

A bathroom in the French Empire style. The bold checkered colorwashing on the walls (see pages 78–83) echoed by the tiled floor, creates an atmosphere of romance and sophistication. The same technique has been used to decorate the bath, throwing the white legs into relief.
(LEFT)

Vertical stripes, the graceful curves of painted Moorish designs, and a cool color scheme of pale, muted greens and greenish whites all help to offset the narrowness of this corridor-like space.
(RIGHT)

Yellow can be a very successful bathroom color. Here, it prevents the greenish white of the cupboards from becoming cold, and provides a warm foil for the painted tortoiseshell-patterned chair (see pages 116–17).
(FAR RIGHT, BELOW)

The combination of yellow and white has a classical grace all its own, and enhances the spacious proportions of this bathroom. The bold splashes of burnt sienna encircling the window over the bath and decorating the floor divider give the recessed bath area its own separate identity.

(ABOVE)

EXTERIORS

A tough, hardwearing finish may be your principal aim when painting the outside of a building, but don't overlook the opportunity for a truly stunning exterior. The colors and effects you use will be dictated largely by the climate you live in and the shape, proportion, and period of the building. Generally, bright color looks best on doors and windows in cool, indirect light, and on walls in sunnier climates. Wooden buildings can often take stronger colors than brick or stone.

Bright azure colorwash on plaster walls (see pages 78–83) enhances this traditional rural building. The vibrant color highlights the silver-gray timberwork, and is balanced by the natural, mellow tones of the roof tiles and wooden door.
(ABOVE)

Distressed furniture complements the simple elegance of this wooden porch. The muted gray shade of the building has enough blue in it to prevent the color becoming flat, but is crisp enough to act as a foil for the soft greens of the surrounding landscape.
(LEFT)

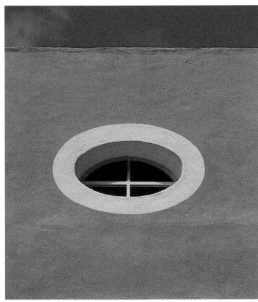

The rust-red of this traditional wooden dwelling in Connecticut has an
exciting intensity. The vivid blue and green colors of the shutters, glimpsed
through the window panes, break up the solid geometry of the building and
prevent the mass of red from becoming too overwhelming.

(ABOVE)

A small, round window can be lost in a large wall. This one is greatly
enhanced by its broad white frame and white glazing bars. Dark bars would
have rendered the window a black hole; white bars without a
supporting frame would have appeared spindly and insubstantial.

(LEFT)

A warm ochre earth color applied over textured walls enhances the natural beauty of this stone wall coping and doorway.
(ABOVE)

An anonymous passageway has been enlivened by painting the inner wall in broken pink. The color also helps to create a sense of progression, drawing the eye through to the courtyard beyond.
(LEFT)

Each of the horizontal panels in these double doors has been treated as a separate design opportunity. The exuberant mass of rectangles has been been paired off in carefully alternating colors. This kind of vivid decoration is particularly successful in hot, sunny climates, and looks good when juxtaposed with other strong colors.

(ABOVE)

Freehand figurative designs in a variety of warm tones have been used to enliven the entrance to this wooden house. Wit and humor link the diverse elements: the red door can be viewed as a face, the sunburst on the portico as "hair."

(LEFT)

FROM COLORWASHING AND SPONGING TO
WOODGRAINING AND MARBLING, PAINT EFFECTS CAN BE
USED TO ENHANCE ALMOST ANY SURFACE. SURPRISINGLY,
THEY ARE OFTEN SIMPLE TO CREATE.

techniques and effects

DESPITE THEIR DIVERSITY, decorative paint techniques can be grouped into three main families. The first is "broken color," which refers to the application of one or more colors in semi-transparent layers over a different base color. These layers can be partly wiped off or manipulated in other ways to provide pattern and texture. The  *second is "antiquing," whereby various methods are used to give surfaces and objects the look of mellowed age. The final group is "faux finishes:" using paint to imitate different materials such as marble or wood. At its most advanced, this also includes the sophisticated technique of painting optical illusions, otherwise known as trompe l'oeil.*

These various paint effects do have one thing in common: because they are all carried out by hand, the finished result will always be absolutely unique, giving the objects or surfaces that you decorate a truly personal touch.

Distressed colorwashes of burnt sienna and yellow ochre
applied in a harlequin diamond pattern give the narrow twist of
this stairway a dramatic sense of height and depth.

BROKEN COLOR

Colorwashing

A light green glaze brushed loosely over a pale yellow base. The resulting patchy effect gives these walls a much softer appearance than evenly applied layers of a single color.
(BELOW)

An elegant way to enhance interior walls, colorwashing consists of applying a coat of thinned, sometimes translucent, paint (the "glaze") over a white or colored background ("the base color"). Three types of paint can be used: oil-based, which usually gives the greatest depth to the color; water-based latex or acrylic paints, which give a flatter color but dry rapidly; and distemper, which, although not widely available, can be made at home (see page 201).

Colorwashes can be given a variety of different textures and patterns by distressing the surface: either by brushing on or wiping off additional coats or by using one of the broken-color techniques described in this chapter. You can use any combination of colors on a distressed wall, but it is generally unwise to mix too many different shades because you may lose control of the variety and end up with a stormy sky when you wanted a cool glow. Always test out your finish on a piece of cardboard or a patch of wall before you start.

Colorwashing with oil-based paint

PREPARATION

A properly primed plaster wall should be given a coat of undercoat followed by two coats of the base color. Eggshell paint gives the smoothest finish while providing enough texture or key for the color-washing on top. Always allow the base coats to dry for at least 24 hours before applying the colorwash.

APPLICATION

Oil-based paints can be thinned up to 1:1 with paint thinner. Adding more solvent will give the finish greater translucency but the paint thinner may separate out from the paint overnight, so avoid mixing any more than you can use in a day. Flat oil paint (see page 163) mixed 1:8 parts paint to paint thinner, gives a firm, even wash with some degree of depth. If it is thinned down any further than this it will become translucent, but the increased unevenness of the coat will produce a mottled effect. In certain cases this may be desirable, but should be avoided if you want an even finish.

Undercoat can also be thinned to 1:8 parts paint to paint thinner and used as a wash over a base coat of undiluted under-coat, or over eggshell if you want a flat effect of some depth. However, it does not have the same color qualities as flat oil paint and the finish will appear somewhat powdery by comparison. Eggshell paint, thinned to 1:8 parts paint to paint thinner and used as a wash, gives a less even effect than flat oil paint but provides better color quality than undercoat.

Apply all the above mixes using a soft, wide brush, working carefully and steadily and finishing off all your strokes toward the light to prevent a patchy effect. When using oil-based paints, always leave at least 24 hours drying time between each coat of colorwash.

DISTRESSING

Oil-based paint can be used for distressed effects but is best thinned down up to 1:1 with paint thinner. Drying times between coats will consequently shorten to 8–12 hours. Apply each coat with a broad brush, using loose, criss-cross strokes. If you want to soften the effect, use a dry brush as you work. Once the first coat is dry, apply the next in the same way and allow to dry. Two distressing coats will normally be suffi-cient; additional coats will gradually even out the mottled effect.

FINISHING

It is imperative that a distressed surface be protected with at least one coat of matte or eggshell oil-based varnish, because the thinning of the paint and the patchiness of its application make it particularly vulnerable to damage. Varnish has the additional benefit of distributing light more evenly over a surface, giving it an appear-ance of greater depth.

An oil-based color-wash gives these walls great lucidity and depth. The look is complemented by the distressed woodwork, where white paint has been sanded off to reveal layers of blue-green paint and bare wood beneath.

(ABOVE)

Apply the latex base coat with regular strokes for an even finish, or criss-cross strokes for a more mottled effect. (TOP)

Brush on the second color—a diluted wash—with criss-cross strokes, to achieve a patchy, cloudy look. (ABOVE)

For a subtle glow of golden color, overlay a pale yellow latex base with a diluted wash (1:3 parts paint to water) tinted with burnt sienna and yellow ochre. (RIGHT)

Colorwashing with water-based paint

PREPARATION

If you are working straight onto plaster, a latex colorwash should be applied over two coats of latex base color, the first coat thinned to 3:1 parts paint to water and the second at full strength. Allow this base coat to dry for at least 24 hours before color-washing. If you are painting over old paint, first wash it down, wipe with a water-and-vinegar solution to remove any grease and rinse thoroughly. Allow to dry before color-washing. Latex paint can be thinned up to 1:3 parts paint to water, or 1:4 if you want to make it translucent.

APPLICATION

The most transparent water-based color-wash is a mixture of pure pigment and water, with the addition of a very small amount of latex paint to give it a little body

and to bind it (otherwise it might rub off the walls). Add about 2 tablespoons of paint per 2 pints (1 litre) of water. If you want a stronger tint, add a little artist's gouache—taking care not to overdo it as the coloring effect is very strong—then test it out on a piece of cardboard pre-coated with the base color. Make sure that the pigments are well mixed to avoid streakiness.

For a translucent colorwash, dilute the latex to 1:4 parts paint to water. Apply this mixture liberally and briskly using a soft, wide brush. It's a good idea to keep a dry brush or sponge at hand to mop up any drips. For a colorwash with a little more body but less transparency, use a 1:3 ratio of paint to water. If you want an even finish, cross off all your final strokes toward the light.

DISTRESSING

Water-based paint is usually considered the best medium for distressing interior walls, and should ideally be applied over other water-based or acrylic paints. A water-based colorwash will dry quickly and leave a soft, cloud-like finish. Apply it liberally and loosely, brushing in all directions and leaving some areas of the base coat uncovered or only very lightly coated. Leave this to dry for 24 hours before applying the next coat. Paint this thinly and evenly over the surface so that the distressed patches show through: this will enrich the color of the first coat while softening the appearance of the distressed areas. If the wash runs, work it in with a sponge or brush. You can apply any number of coats you like, but keep in mind the more you apply, the darker the final color will become and the less mottled and translucent the finish.

FINISHING

As for oil-based colorwashes, a coat or two of matte or eggshell, this time acrylic, varnish is advisable for distressed surfaces.

Colorwashing with distemper

Distemper finishes are similar to those created with latex paint, but they are less hardwearing and have a softer, grainier appearance which can be very subtle.

PREPARATION

There are three basic kinds of distemper: ready-made oil-bound distemper; soft distemper, a mixture of whiting and size; and casein or milk-based distemper (see page 201 for recipes). Distemper is particularly suitable for use on uneven surfaces, and all of the above can be applied over any sound surface already painted with latex paint provided it is clean and dry, but do not use it on a surface that is already covered with old distemper. For the base coat, distemper should be the consistency of standard latex, but for the wash coat or coats thin it down to the consistency of milk.

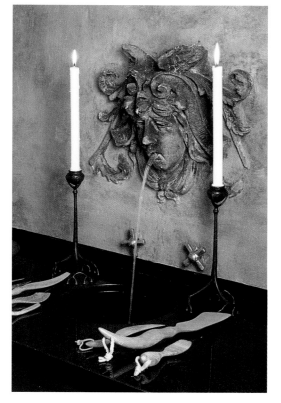

APPLICATION

Distemper dries very quickly. If you are using soft distemper, you can lengthen its drying time by adding 1 tablespoon of glycerine per 2 pints (1 litre).

Close all doors and windows to prevent the paint from drying out too fast and apply the distemper liberally and quickly, starting at the window side of the room and working inward. Finish off each stroke towards the light. If you miss a portion of wall, touch it up with a sponge: brushstrokes are difficult to blend once they have started to dry. As soon as you have finished, open the doors and windows to get the air circulating. You will need between one and three coats, depending on the effect required. Allow 24 hours for drying between coats.

FINISHING

If you apply a final coat of varnish over distemper you will lose the delicate effect. For this reason, distemper is best left unsealed.

The perfect backdrop for an elaborate "antique" molding, these walls have been distressed with a distemper colorwash in two neutral gray-blue tones, gently rubbed with a cloth while still wet.
(LEFT)

The heavier finish of these walls was achieved by applying a dark terracotta wash patchily over a paler base color with broad, quick brushstrokes.
(BELOW LEFT)

Colorwashing with glazes

Scumble glaze washes can be used to give a glowing translucency to walls. As an alternative to thinned, oil-based paint, you can use oil-based glaze tinted with artist's pigments, flat oil paint, undercoat or eggshell. Proprietary glazes vary in consistency; thin them with paint thinner according to the manufacturer's instructions. The more solvent you add, the quicker the glaze will dry. Water-based acrylic scumble glazes are used in a similar way and can be applied over either oil- or water-based paints, although to different effect.

For a smooth, translucent effect, apply an oil-based glaze evenly over the base color in vertical, parallel strokes using a soft, wide brush. (TOP)

For a more mottled finish, apply with loose, criss-cross strokes. (ABOVE)

This subtle sheen of blue is created by brushing a light ultramarine oil-based glaze unevenly over a pale sky-blue base. (RIGHT)

Oil-based glaze

Oil-based glazes, or glazing media, can be applied over the same base color preparation as described for oil-based paints (see page 79). They can be tinted with either artist's oil pigments, flat oil paint, undercoat, or eggshell paint. If you are tinting the glaze with artist's pigments, dilute the pigment first in some paint thinner, and then stir it gradually and thoroughly into the glaze. Start by thinning the glaze with paint thinner until you get the effect you want, then test out the color on a piece of cardboard pre-coated with the base color before you start working directly onto the surface.

APPLICATION

Tinted, oil-based glazes dry rapidly in comparison to oil-based paints. Apply these glazes in even, parallel strokes using a soft 3½in (9cm) brush and working in a downward motion. Work briskly but without rushing. This technique will be easier if you first practice the strokes on a piece of card or on a part of the wall that is to be over-painted. Oil-based glaze gives a fine, translucent depth rarely achievable with diluted paint, but it is trickier to apply evenly. Do not overbrush an area of glaze more than a minute after applying it, as this will cause streaks.

DISTRESSING

Oil-based glaze gives a sharper appearance than distressing using diluted oil-based paint. The patches dry faster and the final effect resembles foggy stained glass rather than mottled stone. Apply the oil-based glaze using loose, criss-cross strokes. It is worth practicing on a piece of board before you start until you get the type of effect you want.

FINISHING

Because oil-based glaze is similar to varnish, it is not strictly necessary to apply a finishing coat. However, a final layer of matte or satin varnish is recommended. This will give the surface an even finish, which enhances the mottling of the color without highlighting the surface variation of the glaze where it catches the light.

Acrylic scumble glaze

PREPARATION

Acrylic scumble glazes have a slightly foggy white tone in their concentrated form, and although this rarely shows once they are applied, it does have a cooling effect on color. They can be applied over latex paints, but could also be used over oil-based paint, provided it is thoroughly dry and grease free.

Acrylic glazes can be tinted with artist's acrylic pigments, artist's gouache, latex paints, or universal tints. Colorants can either be mixed with a little water and then added to the glaze, or applied to it directly. The first option gives you more control over the final color, but you should avoid over-thinning the glaze. As with oil-based glaze, mix in the colorant gradually and thoroughly, testing the color on a piece of cardboard to ensure that there are no lumps of undiluted pigment which will create streaks on the wall. Acrylic scumble glazes can be mixed 1:1 with artist's acrylics to give a very transparent finish (although they may give a cloudy tint to pale colors). They may then be diluted up to 3:1 parts glaze to water. If you would rather tint the glaze with latex paint, a mix of 7 parts glaze, 2 parts latex and 1 part water is a good balance.

Unlike latex paints, acrylic glazes are ideal for creating distressed finishes on domestic woodwork such as doors and baseboards. You can work over any smooth, sound surface, provided it is clean, dry, and grease free.

APPLICATION

Apply as for oil-based glazes (see page 82). Acrylic dries rapidly, so avoid overbrushing areas of glaze that have been in place for over a minute. If you get streaks and patches, do not try to blend them in; wipe off the glaze completely and start again. Although acrylic dries quickly, allow at least 24 hours before reapplying.

DISTRESSING

As for oil-based glazes, acrylics should be applied using loose, criss-cross strokes. Practice on a piece of cardboard or patch of wall before you start until you get the type of effect you want.

FINISHING

Because acrylic scumble glaze is similar to varnish it is not strictly necessary to apply a finishing coat. However, as for oil-based glazes, a matte or satin varnish will give the surface an even finish without highlighting the surface variation of the glaze where it catches the light.

These plaster walls have been decorated with a series of delicately colored glazes, sanded off vigorously when dry for an "antique" finish. (BELOW)

Shading

This is a technique in which different shades of a color are blended across a surface to create a transition from dark to light. It is often used subtly to balance out the distribution of natural light in a room.

Shading not only adjusts the light effects in a room but can also give the appearance of altering its proportions. Using a pale tone on the lower walls and progressively darker shades as you work upward will visually lower a very high ceiling. If the process is reversed, with darker tones used lower down the walls and lighter shades on the ceiling, the height of the room will be increased. Blank areas of bare wall can be "softened" if they are painted in gradually darkening shades, working out from the center.

Interesting effects can also be achieved by applying several different colors, although you should avoid using too many.

These delicate color gradations were achieved using four tones of viridian green oil-based paint, brushed on vertically over a white base coat. The colors were softly blended into one another with vertical strokes from a broad, dry brush and were given a final sealing coat of satin oil-based varnish. (RIGHT)

Before starting work, give yourself some indication of how the colors will appear by painting the color transitions you want on a piece of cardboard and holding it up in front of the area you wish to paint.

Shading with oil-based paint

Flat oil paint is an ideal choice for this technique. A high-quality, versatile paint, it covers a much greater area than the popular commercial paints, although it is a little harder to use. Flat oil paint can usually be found in specialist trade suppliers. If you have problems finding a supplier, eggshell paint can be used as a substitute. Buy a large can in the palest color you are likely to use and tint it yourself.

PREPARATION

Apply one or more layers of flat oil paint or undercoat as a base coat, thinning the last coat with a mixture of 1:2 parts linseed oil to paint thinner. This will give the paint enough sheen to allow easy manipulation of the shading coats over it.

In general, you will need to mix four shades for a large wall and three for a smaller area; however, if your room is unusually large you may need five shades. Mix the darkest shade first, followed by the lightest, before working on the middle shades. Dissolve some artist's oil-based pigment in a little paint thinner, mixing it with a palette knife. Add the pigment solution to the flat oil paint, stirring constantly to ensure that the pigment is evenly distributed. Proceed with caution, as artist's pigments are surprisingly strong and they will change the color of the flat oil paint rapidly. Once you are happy with the colors, thin the paint with a mixture of 1:3 parts linseed oil to paint thinner. The paint thinner will make it easier to blend each shade into the next, the linseed oil will prevent the paint from drying too quickly or becoming too thin. Do not apply any of your shades until they are all mixed and ready to use.

MARKING OUT A WALL

Before applying the shading coats, mark at the top of the wall approximately where you intend your shading transitions to occur, dividing up the space according to how many shades you are using. Light blue chalk is best for this because it vanishes most easily beneath paint. Roll a length of twine in the blue chalk and attach a small weight to one end.

If you are shading across a wall from one end to the other, suspend the twine vertically from each mark in turn and snap the line tightly against the wall to leave a blue chalk line. Indicate which shade is to be used in each band. If you are shading a wall horizontally from top to bottom, draw along a level or get someone else to hold one end of the chalk-covered twine horizontally while you snap it against the wall from the other end to leave a line. Indicate the position of the different shades as before.

APPLICATION

When applying shading, always start with the palest color and work towards the darkest. At each transition, brush the lighter color into the next using an ordinary brush. Change the brush at least once to avoid spreading too much of one shade into the next, or use a separate brush for each color. Then go over the roughly blended area with a stippling brush, followed by a sponge, to soften the effect further. The whole process is made much easier if you work with a partner, one person laying on the color while the other follows behind with the stippler and sponge. However, avoid exchanging tasks because no two people's techniques are exactly the same.

Shading with latex paint

Latex paints are best suited to shading small areas, where they can be used to produce a very delicate, soft effect. Shading over a large area with water-based paints can be difficult unless you have a great deal of experience in manipulating both paint and color. The paint tends to dry out before you can blend one tone into another, leaving obvious tide-marks. This can be avoided if you mix a large number of close tones from light to dark and work very fast, applying narrow bands of color while a partner follows immediately behind, stippling or sponging across each transition. If you do attempt it, first prime the wall with a coat of eggshell to make it less absorbent.

A successful use of muted shading, with the colors applied in horizontal bands. Shading with darker colors can often resemble dirt or discoloration, but using color tones that are clearly distinct from one another helps to offset this tendency.
(ABOVE)

Sponging

This is one of the easiest and most enjoyable of all the broken-color techniques. You can forget about drying times, keeping a wet edge workable, closing doors and windows, finishing off brushstrokes towards the light, and dealing with sticky glazes, and, if you use oil-based paint, you can wipe off anything you don't like and start all over again.

Sponging with latex paints gives a soft, cloudy effect, with very delicate shifts of color. Oil-based paints produce a crisper texture that can resemble granite or porphyry, while oil glazes give translucent, marble-like finishes.

MATERIALS AND EQUIPMENT

You will need a sloping, roller-type paint tray with a reservoir at one end, a piece of cardboard, a clean undyed rag and, of course, a sponge. Genuine sea sponges are the best type to use, as they are very pliable and their irregular shape ensures that the patterns they leave are never repetitive. They also hold paint better than synthetic sponges. However, cellulose sponges are quite adequate provided you tear them first with the help of scissors and turn them round constantly as you work. Before use, wash a sea sponge in water, squeeze it out and then dip into paint thinner if using oil-based paint, water if latex. Allow the sponge to dry out and return to its full size before you start work.

APPLICATION

Dab the sponge lightly into the paint on the tray and test it out first on the piece of cardboard, removing any excess paint, until you get the impression you want. Do this each time you load the sponge with paint and before working directly onto the surface to be decorated. You will soon get to know the feel of the correct paint load.

Sponging with oil- or water-based glazes gives a translucent finish. The oil-based glazes have more depth, while the water-based glazes have a greater softness. You can experiment with thinner glazes, but do be careful not to thin them too much, or you will end up with a runny blot.

Sponging on and sponging off

There are two main types of sponge-patterning techniques: the conventional method, in which paint is applied with the sponge, and the reductive method, in which the sponge is used to apply solvent, removing part of a paint layer to reveal a different color beneath. While the former method produces a series of colors which appear to float upwards from some depth, the latter gives a softer, mottled effect.

Most conventional sponging methods use two to four colors, either in various shades

These bedroom walls have been decorated with a sponging technique, resulting in a delicate bloom of color. A pale pink base color was over-sponged with a coat of deeper pink, followed by two successively lighter shades to increase the sense of depth. (BELOW)

Before you start "sponging on," test the basic technique on cardboard to get a feel for how much paint to use. It is best to do this every time you re-coat the sponge with paint, and before working directly onto the surface. (LEFT)

This finish has been created using the "sponging on" technique, and the final effect has depth and movement. A dark cobalt blue was applied liberally over a very pale blue-white base, and topped with a final layer of paler (thinned) cobalt blue. (LEFT)

Working over a pale, evenly applied base, sponge on the first, darkest color, dabbing it on gently and spreading it well. (ABOVE)

When the first coat has dried, sponge on a second, paler layer using the same technique, irregularly overlapping the first. (ABOVE)

of the same color or in contrasting tones. Always apply lighter colors over darker ones, as this gives a greater sense of depth. If you wish to sponge across both walls and woodwork in the same room, avoid using the same color for the two different surfaces.

Sponging woodwork

Delicate pieces of furniture, such as chairs with thin legs, should be sponged with oil-based paint, because the very soft finish of water-based paints will not show up. In contrast, large, solid objects will benefit from the mottled effect of water-based paints, provided that you protect the finish with a coat of varnish.

Use a damp sponge to remove a little of the glaze. (ABOVE)

"Sponging off" produces a softer effect than "sponging on." An evenly applied cobalt and ultramarine glaze was here dabbed off with a damp sponge to reveal the base color. (LEFT)

Spattering

Spattering is one of the most exciting and attractive of broken-color effects. Its apparent simplicity, however, is deceptive. It takes far more control than the techniques of sponging, stippling or ragging and is also extremely messy, so you should take care to cover anything which you don't want given instant measles—including yourself. Color is the key to successful spattering, and provided you have a clear idea of what you want, you will find that boldness always pays off.

MATERIALS AND EQUIPMENT

A stiff brush is essential for spattering, preferably a stenciler which has short, squared-off bristles. You will also need a straight-edged piece of wood, water- or oil-based paint, solvent, and some paper already painted in your chosen base color. The paint should be no thicker than milk in consistency, while if it is any thinner you risk it running down the walls in streaks. Experiment until you get the paint to the right color and texture, then practice your spattering movement until you feel confident enough to begin.

A pale wall with a delicate sprinkling of dark spots finds a negative image in the mantelpiece below, with its fine white flecks spattered over deep slate gray.
(RIGHT)

APPLICATION

There are two main methods of spreading a spatter, neither of which involves wrist flicking. If you want medium-sized spots, about ¼in (6mm) in diameter, load the brush lightly with paint at the tip, stand about 12in (30cm) away from your target surface and use the straight-edged piece of wood to strike the brush at the base of the head with a sharp, chopping stroke. Avoid flicking the brush up as you do this or you will end up spattering your face instead. If you want bigger spots, hold the brush and wood closer to the target.

For a speckled finish, spatter vermilion, cerulean blue and indigo acrylic paints from a stiff brush by running a steel comb across the bristles. Wait until each layer is dry before you begin the next. The larger spots are made by striking the brush on a straight-edge about 18in (45cm) from the surface. To finish, seal with eggshell acrylic varnish. (LEFT)

The spattering action involves striking the shaft of the loaded brush using a straight-edged piece of wood. The nearer you stand to your surface, the larger the spots will be. (ABOVE)

You can create clear bands within the spattering pattern by sticking masking tape onto the surface before you begin. Remove the tape when the paint has dried. (ABOVE)

For slightly more controlled spattering and smaller spots, try holding the brush, bristles upward, about 8in (20cm) away from the target surface and run a comb or your finger across the bristles and toward you in a single, even stroke. With practice, you will be able to aim the flight and fall of your droplets with accuracy.

If you intend to apply a second layer of spatters, keep the first layer fairly open or you will risk overcrowding the spots. Using lighter-colored dots over darker ones will give a somewhat three-dimensional effect.

Ceilings can be spattered by holding the straight-edge above the brush and chopping the brush upward against it. Stand a little closer to the surface to allow for gravity.

SAFETY PRECAUTIONS

If you are spattering above your head it is essential to wear a mask and goggles or, at the very least, an old pair of sunglasses and a rag over your nose and mouth. Most modern decorating paints present little risk so long as they are kept out of the mouth and eyes, but flat oil paint can cause minor skin irritation, even after it is scrubbed off. If you have sensitive skin and are likely to be in contact with oil-based and some acrylic paints, wear rubber gloves and cover any exposed areas of skin.

Ragrolling and Ragging

Most ragrolling and ragging involves painting a colored glaze over a base coat and then distressing the surface with a rag or cloth. The technique can be used to make a surface look as crisp as polished stone or as soft as crushed velvet, depending on the types of fabric and paint used. Off-white or pale backgrounds generally work best; darker ragged surfaces can look very heavy.

For ragrolling, a rag is folded into a sausage shape of varying tightness and then rolled across a glazed surface. All kinds of materials can be used to produce different textures. For ragging, a piece of cloth is crumpled up and pressed repeatedly against a glazed surface to produce a sharper effect than ragrolling. Both patterns are endlessly variable, but ragrolling tends to have a sense of movement in its pattern, while ragging appears more static.

WHERE TO RAG AND ROLL

Ragrolling is better suited to walls and ceilings than it is to furniture, although it can look good used on flat surfaces such as table-tops and cupboards, or panels that are part of the main wall area. Areas to avoid completely are doors, windows, and their frames. The moldings on such surfaces make them difficult to work on and the results are generally unsuccessful.

Ragging is ideal for camouflaging objects such as radiators, which will virtually disappear if given the same ragged finish as the wall behind. Large items of furniture like chests of drawers can be ragged but it is best to use the softer effects; sharp ragging can look too dominant, sometimes completely breaking up the visual structure of an object. The technique is ideal for enhancing anonymous areas, incorporating oddly proportioned alcoves into a room, and giving a fresh look to large, bland areas.

RAGGING EFFECTS

Apart from their versatility and elegance, ragging and ragrolling techniques are popular because they are fast and simple to carry out. To achieve the elegant look of white damask fabric, mix some white paint with a trace of black and rag or ragroll it over an off-white background. Alternatively, rolling white or the palest blue-gray over a stone gray ground will give the effect of crushed white velvet.

Experiment with different fabrics to produce a whole range of textures: rolling burlap, linen, and cheesecloth over an ochre

An amber glaze ragged over a creamy base color makes a gently textured foil for a stripped and distressed cupboard. (BELOW)

and pale yellow ground will, respectively, give the look of leather, parchment, and fine wool. Net curtaining rolled over a thin glaze can, paradoxically, give the effect of linen or canvas, whereas linen can be rolled over different colors to resemble polished stone—one of the primary techniques of faux marbling.

MATERIALS AND EQUIPMENT

Use the same types of paint mixed to the same consistencies as those for sponging (see page 86). Unless you are using water-based paint, you will need plenty of solvent and a large amount of your selected rag.

APPLICATION

If you are using oil-based paints and glazes, it is generally best to apply the layer to be ragged over a darker base color. This can be laid on in wider bands than the 2ft (60cm) strips used for stippling (see page 95). If you are ragrolling, roll the sausage of rag down and across the surface in a gentle motion as though you were picking up flour on a roll of pastry. Try this out first on lining paper or a piece of cardboard until you get the movement right. Leave about 6in (15cm) unragged at the edge of each band of glaze, ragging over the join as you add each additional band. In constricted areas such as corners, the edges of dados or baseboards, blend the last inch or so by dabbing with a sponge.

If you are using latex paint or acrylic scumble glazes, both of which dry very fast, you will need to modify your approach. Apply the paint in narrower bands and rag immediately over the area. This is easier to do with a partner, one laying on the color, the other ragging. If you want to apply a second ragged layer over the first, make sure that the first layer is dry before you start. As with the base coat, the second layer should be lighter in color than the first, but experimental variations with light and dark colors can often be successful.

A translucent, clean glaze layer applied over ragging looks handsome, but take care to finish this unbroken top coat with downward brushstrokes to avoid a cross-hatching effect. Finish ragged furniture with satin varnish; avoid matte varnish, which makes ragged wood look like cardboard, and high gloss, which obscures the finish.

Ragrolling downwards over a glazed surface. (ABOVE)

Brush indigo oil-based glaze evenly over a pale blue base. Rag-roll off with a downward motion. (LEFT)

Ragging with a crumpled pad of cloth. Press the pad firmly but gently against the glazed surface, then remove without leaving a downward smear. (ABOVE)

Apply burgundy-red acrylic glaze evenly over a pale cream base, then gently rag off. Re-crumpling the rag at intervals will give the pattern more variety. (ABOVE LEFT)

Dragging or Strié

Dragging is a freer use of the woodgraining technique (see pages 112–15) and produces a softer, more informal effect. It is carried out by drawing a dry brush down through wet glaze so that the base color is revealed beneath fine, irregularly spaced lines, producing the appearance of woven fabric or planed, close-grained wood. If a second glaze layer is then applied and dragged horizontally—at right-angles to the first—the

texture will be similar to that of a heavy woven fabric. If the glaze is applied in different directions and both coats are dragged vertically, you can produce the look of watered silk. Pastel colors are most suitable for all dragging techniques.

Since dragging always produces a graining effect, it is ideal for use on woodwork such as doors, baseboards and furniture, but be sure to follow the natural line of the grain. Doors should be dragged in the same sequence as that described for painting them (see page 199). The joints in a paneled door can be emphasized by using a slightly darker color than the glazing tone, or a fine score mark filled with pencil lead.

Any wall or surface that is to be dragged in one direction must be as smooth as possible, as any bumps or pits will inevitably be exaggerated by the dragging process. Always make the finishing stroke of the glaze application downward to avoid patchy build-ups.

PAINT

An oil-based top coat applied over a layer of undercoat and dragged will produce an opaque, softly merging effect that is slow to dry. If you use a base coat of either flat oil paint, undercoat or eggshell, and drag in a layer of thinned eggshell top coat, you will get a translucent finish with a fast drying time. Dragging an oil-based glaze on the same base will give sharp, semi-opaque definition, but will take a long time to dry. Although it does not adhere as well, you can also drag in wet latex paint over eggshell to produce a soft, delicate finish which dries very quickly indeed.

*To give wood an antique appearance, apply
a purple-indigo glaze over a base color using a
broad dragger. Before the glaze is dry, distress the
surface with a stiff rag or paper. When the glaze
has dried, scratch into the surface.*
(LEFT)

APPLICATION

As with shading, dragging over a large area is easiest if you work with a partner, one laying on the glaze and the other carrying out the dragging immediately behind. Avoid alternating the jobs as this will disrupt the final effect: no two people will have exactly the same dragging technique. Apply the glaze in 2ft (60cm) wide bands, and leave about 6in (15cm) undragged at the edge of each band until the next glaze area has been brushed into it. Wipe the dragging brush

First apply a base coat and allow to dry. Paint on a coat of glaze and immediately draw a dry brush lightly but steadily downwards through the glaze. (ABOVE)

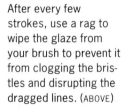

After every few strokes, use a rag to wipe the glaze from your brush to prevent it from clogging the bristles and disrupting the dragged lines. (ABOVE)

after every few strokes to prevent it from clogging up with glaze. It is important that the glaze is "alive"—not stiff and tacky—before you drag. If it has started to dry out, wipe off the glaze promptly with solvent and start again. Adding a further layer of glaze on top of a tacky patch will leave a dark mark.

Unless you have a very steady hand or are a seasoned decorator, you may find that applying dragging strokes in straight, vertical lines takes some practice. For dragging, hold the brush by its handle, resting the shaft in your hand as you would a pen, and try to keep the action fairly loose-wristed.

For this effect, paint on a base coat of duck-egg blue flat oil paint sealed with clear eggshell varnish. Using a broad brush, apply emerald green eggshell thinned to 4:1 parts paint to paint thinner. While still wet, drag with a clean brush using single vertical strokes. Seal with clear varnish. (LEFT)

Gripping the handle too tightly will result in wobbly lines. Rest the tips of the bristles against the wall and, in one stroke, lightly and steadily slide the brush downwards. If you still feel unconfident and doubt that you can drag straight, hang a plumbline from the ceiling and follow it down. Alternatively, hammer a few nails into a straight-edge and position it so that the flat heads of the nails hold the wood just away from the wall, then use the edge as a guide. You can make horizontal strokes the same way, first checking that the straight-edge is even using a level. If you find it is impossible to make a single downward stroke from ceiling to baseboard, stop the stroke below waist height and then work upward from the floor, softening the join with a soft, dry brush or a clean cloth. Vary the level of the join along the wall or you may get a ripple effect, but always keep it below eye level.

Combing

Like dragging, combing is a simplified version of woodgraining (see pages 112–15) and produces a sharp, stylized pattern. It consists of running a comb through wet glaze. Any comb will do, whether it is a hair comb, a rubber-toothed three-sided comb designed specially for this purpose, or any serrated edge with regular or irregular teeth. Whatever the tool, the effect will always be sharp. As a result, it is possible to use two contrasting colors to great effect.

PAINT

Oil-based paint is most suitable for combing techniques. Combing in an oil-based top coat over a layer of undercoat produces a fine, crisp effect. The combinations of glazes and base coats described for dragging (see pages 92–3) are also suitable for combing, but latex paints are not suitable for this technique.

A triangular rubber comb with irregular teeth can be used to create sinuous wavy lines. (TOP)

A stiffer rubber or metal comb is better for drawing sharp parallel or checked patterns. In both cases, the teeth of the comb should be kept at near right-angles to the surface. (ABOVE)

Brush a vermilion acrylic glaze evenly over an emerald base coat. Immediately draw a stiff triangular rubber comb with irregular teeth down through the glaze to reveal the base color. (RIGHT)

APPLICATION

Although combing is, in essence, a simple procedure, it is another broken-color technique that is easiest to do if you work with a partner: follow the method described for dragging (see page 93). You may also find it helpful to employ a straight-edge or plumbline as a guide to keep your hand steady as you work.

FLOORS

Combing is an ideal technique for decorating floors. At the most basic level, you can simply follow the grain of the floorboards, but there is plenty of scope for creating patterns, for example, emulating the effect of straw matting. On floors it is essential to use flat oil paint, undercoat or eggshell paint, which will last for years if properly protected by three coats of polyurethane varnish or five coats of more traditional varnish. Specially-made floor paints are available, but unfortunately they come in a very limited color range.

Prime new wood, then apply a full-strength undercoat followed by at least two slightly thinned layers of your colored base coat. The combing coat should be a mixture of 3:1 parts glaze to paint thinner . It may go without saying, but you should always work toward the door. If you are combing a floor pattern with any geometric design, copy the design onto paper first and divide it up into a grid of regular squares. Using chalk, draw another grid directly onto the floor and transfer the pattern, taking the grid as a guide. Straight-edged patterns, where one direction of combing ends and another begins in the opposite direction, should be combed with masking tape along the edges, and worked over in a checkerboard manner, the alternating areas being filled in when the others are dry. Once you have finished combing, protect your work with three coats of protective polyurethane varnish.

Stippling

Stippling is carried out using a large, flat-faced, relatively soft-bristled brush known as a stippler. This is dabbed onto wet glaze, removing just enough of it to allow the base coat to show through. The process produces a fine, mottled texture similar to lemon peel.

Stippling brushes can be expensive and if you are decorating a small area, shoe brushes or even hairbrushes make good substitutes. For large or awkward areas such as stairwells, where an even finish is not necessary, a worn broom on a long handle will do.

PAINT

A variety of both oil- and water-based paints are suitable for stippling. Stippling a transparent or semi-transparent glaze that has been applied over a white or light-colored ground gives an elegant effect similar to that of pastel chalk rubbed over lightly tinted paper. Using a glaze also slows down the drying process, giving you more time to work. Alternatively, applying a coat of oil-based flat paint over a ground of eggshell and then stippling it gives surfaces an iridescent quality.

Stippling works well over both large and small surfaces; use it to create precise patterns on table-tops or other furniture, with masking tape as a guide. Stippled surfaces benefit from being contrasted with another finish such as sponging or stenciling, so avoid carrying the technique across both walls and woodwork without a break.

APPLICATION

First apply a base coat with an ordinary brush and leave it to dry. Then, with another standard brush, lay on oil-based or acrylic glaze thinly and evenly in vertical bands, about 2ft (60cm) wide if working on a wall. Stipple each band immediately after it has been applied. Press the brush face-on onto the surface; the bristle points should strike with a firm but gentle dabbing motion. Never slide the brush or allow the sides of the bristles to touch the glaze. As soon as the tool gets overloaded with glaze, clean it by wiping with a rag dipped in either paint thinner for oil-based glaze or water for acrylic glaze.

Stippling is easier if two people work together, one laying on glaze, the other stippling behind. However, avoid alternating the tasks as the change of stippling touch will disrupt the harmony of the finish. The stippler should leave about 6in (15cm) untouched on the right-hand side of the band (working from left to right) so that the glazer can brush the next stripe into it before the stippler works over the joint. Follow the same principle if you are working alone and avoid stippling the edge of each strip before laying on the next one. If you find you have accidentally put two coats of glaze in one spot, stipple them off with a clean stippler.

Apply an acrylic or oil-based glaze evenly over the base color with a large, flat brush. Dab gently but firmly over the glazed surface with the stippler. If you miss an area of glaze, stipple it on directly rather than applying another layer of glaze and stippling it off. (TOP)

Wipe the stippler occasionally with a rag to prevent glaze clogging the bristles. (ABOVE)

Apply a barley-white base and allow to dry. Brush on a flesh-pink and a pale yellow glaze simultaneously, blending them by using two stipplers in a criss-cross motion. (LEFT)

Lining or Striping

Lining, or striping, consists of painting a band, or lines, of color to enhance the patterns of moldings, to surround an area of marbling or stenciling or, less frequently, to create a graining effect.

MATERIALS

Lining color must flow freely, so the paint used needs to be thin but with a strong pigment density: artist's oil colors, universal tints, and artist's acrylics are the best paints for this technique.

If you are using oil-based paint, dissolve artist's oil pigment or universal tint in paint thinner and a little varnish; the varnish helps the paint dry quicker and makes it just sticky enough to keep the bristles close together and running smoothly. Goldsize or linseed oil can be substituted for the varnish, but the former can be very gluey and the latter is slow to dry. Perfectionists strain the color to prevent any undissolved pigment from producing dark streaks.

When using artist's acrylics, choose the free-flow variety and mix them to the consistency of whole milk. Adding a retarder will slow the drying time, allowing you to wipe off any smudges with a damp sponge.

To apply the paint you will need two artist's brushes, a ⅛–¼in (3–6mm) flat-ended brush for broader lines and a rounded pencil liner for finer ones. Professional decorators use flat-ended hoghair fitches (see page 100) with long, tapering hairs that hold more paint and therefore allow a more controlled stroke, but beginners may find shorter brushes easier to use.

APPLICATION

It is easy to be intimidated by the idea of painting straight lines, but you should remember that in most instances a slight unevenness in the painting only adds to the attractiveness of the final effect.

Before you start painting, mark out the position of your lines with pencil or chalk, being careful to remove any surplus chalk which might be picked up on the lining brush. Light blue chalk is best for this because it vanishes most easily in paint. If you need to join two lines with a curve, follow the method of tracing out drawings used by the fresco painters of the Renaissance. First draw the curve onto a piece of cardboard, then use a darning needle to puncture a row of holes along the line. Place the cardboard in position and brush paint over the holes—a stenciling brush is ideal for this. When you lift off the card, you should be left with a curving

The ochre colorwash of these bedroom walls has been enhanced by a classical Greek lining pattern at dado height and terracotta "paneling." The elongated panel shapes create a feeling of height and spaciousness.
(BELOW)

line of very fine dots. Carefully join up the dots with a pencil liner, resting the little finger of your painting hand against the surface to steady it as you work.

Unless you are working freehand, use a ruler to guide your hand rather than the brush. Turn the ruler so that the beveled surface lies against the wall; this will keep the edge clear of the surface. Resting the middle finger of your brush hand on the straight-edge, steadily move your hand across the surface. For a longer line, glue some corks to one surface of a straight-edge to hold it away from the wall, and follow the edge in the same way as before. Some people prefer to use a string line pinned horizontally or vertically, but you will have to follow it with the head of your brush rather than your hand.

BLOTS AND SLIPS

When using oil-based paint, apply a coat of clear varnish to the surface before lining. This helps the paint to flow easily across the surface and allows you to wipe off any blots and slips using a cloth moistened with paint thinner. An unwanted mark is harder to remove from a semi-porous surface, but if this does occur, try sanding it off gently; take care not to go through the surface beneath, as retouching the ground color almost always shows. If you cannot avoid this, retouch it by feathering the new paint gently into the surrounding area with your finger, sanding it down carefully once dry.

An overloaded brush is the main cause of blots. Press the brush gently against the sides of the paint container to remove any excess and try to apply the paint in a long, single stroke. If you are lining on a wall, start as far up as possible, standing far enough from the wall to give your arm sufficient room for a smooth movement. Try to remain as relaxed as possible—remember, you can always wipe off any mistakes and start again. Rest your hand on the straight-

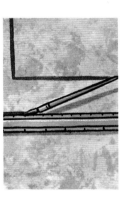

Crimson artist's acrylic paint applied with a pencil liner brush. (ABOVE)

Use a ruler to guide your hand rather than your brush. Turn the ruler beveled side down to keep it clear of the surface you are decorating. (LEFT)

To paint a curved line, first make a stencil by drawing the shape on a piece of cardboard and puncturing tiny holes with a needle. Place the stencil in position and brush over with a stiff stenciling brush loaded with your chosen colour. (TOP)

Join up the dots with a pencil liner, running the brush in a steady curve. To make this easier, rest the little finger of your brush hand against the surface as you work. (ABOVE)

edge and always keep your eye on your hand rather than on the brush.

FINISHING

When you are familiar with the lining technique, try producing an antique effect by thinning down the paint and varying the weight of the lines, so that some are softer than others. Once dry, the lines can be faded and softened by rubbing very lightly with fine sandpaper. Finish the effect with a layer of glaze.

Stenciling

Stenciling is a highly versatile technique which can be used on interior and exterior walls, floors, ceilings, wooden surfaces, fabric, metal and even glass. It is most commonly used as a frieze on walls or a pattern radiating out from the corners, on floors, cupboard doors, and furniture such as chests and stripped or painted chairs, but stenciling can be applied anywhere in a room, so long as vulnerable areas such as floors are protected by varnish. In stenciling, as with other decorative techniques, the simplest schemes are usually the most successful; over-subtle, intricately detailed designs will be lost in a room which has dominating objects and colors.

STENCIL DESIGNS

Ready-cut traditional or contemporary stencils are widely available but it is easy, and much more fun, to make your own. Test out your patterns either by cutting the stencil from colored paper or by drawing it onto a sheet of paper and holding the results up against the surface to be decorated. The two best materials from which to cut stencils are clear acetate and oiled stencil board. When cutting a motif, always cut it from one piece of board or acetate. Never try to join two pieces together—the join will always show up when you paint it.

CUTTING ACETATE

You will need sheets of acetate, a fine artist's pen, masking tape, a surface to cut on—preferably a sheet of glass with masked edges, but hardboard, plywood, or composition board will do—and a scalpel.

Place a sheet of acetate over the design and trace it directly onto the acetate using the pen. Tape the acetate onto the cutting surface. Holding the scalpel firmly, cut steadily towards you without twisting or jerking the blade. Never place your hand in the path of the scalpel: even a slowly moving blade can make a deep wound. When cutting curves, turn the cutting surface rather than your hand. Acetate has an unfortunate tendency to crack or split, particularly when cutting tight curves, but on the whole it is easier to cut than oiled stencil board. Cut small, detailed areas first and, if you are working on glass, do not try to punch them out. Smooth any rough edges with sandpaper.

CUTTING OILED STENCIL BOARD

You will need oiled stencil board, a felt-tipped pen, tracing paper, a hard (3H–5H) pencil, carbon paper, masking tape, a surface to cut on (see Cutting Acetate) and a scalpel.

Stencil board is much cheaper than acetate. It is also thicker, allowing you to bevel the edges to prevent paint from seeping under the stencil. First copy the design onto tracing paper using a fine felt-tipped pen, then transfer it to the oiled board using the hard pencil and carbon paper. Leave a 1–2in (2.5–5cm) margin around the design to ensure that it does not become floppy when cut. Fix the board onto the cutting surface with masking tape and cut it in the same way as for acetate (see left). Bevel the edges by holding the blade at an angle of 45° and cutting outwards, always cutting away from you.

REPEAT MOTIFS

It is best to make one stencil for each color in a repeat motif, moving the stencil along as you work and making sure that you align it correctly. The easiest way to ensure that the stencils are positioned accurately is to cut them out at the same time. Place the stencils one on top of the other, trim them all to the same size and make a small hole at each corner, punching through all the stencils at once. When using the first stencil, make a pencil mark through each hole so that you can position subsequent stencils accurately.

A complex yet graceful stencil pattern in faded indigo on a background of off-white eggshell. The straight lining border prevents the elaborate curves of the stencil from appearing loose and unstructured, and a final coat of eggshell varnish gives the finished design a mellow sheen.
(RIGHT)

If you want to carry your design around a corner, always cut two stencils rather than trying to bend one around the angle, as paint will soon seep under the crease and the stencil itself may break.

PAINT

You can stencil with many different types of paint on virtually any painted or varnished surface, provided that it is level, clean and dry. Gloss paint provides the least key or grip for the paints on top, but applying a layer of matte varnish before stenciling over it will solve the problem, as long as you do not mind losing the shine. Natural wood needs to be sealed with two thinned coats of matte or satin varnish before you start.

Artist's acrylic pigments, thinned if necessary with acrylic medium or water,

latex paint tinted with artist's acrylics or universal tints, and signwriter's colors thinned with paint thinner or matte varnish are all fast-drying and suitable for stenciling on walls. Flat oil paint, undercoat, and egg-shell which have been tinted with artist's oil pigments and thinned with paint thinner are all very effective for use on woodwork, especially when it has been newly primed. All these dry slowly, but the process can be speeded up with drying agents (see page 201). Whatever medium you choose, avoid thinning the paint to a consistency thinner than that of light cream, as it will seep underneath the stencil. You can also use more than one paint color per stencil, if desired, by blending the colors into one another using a technique similar to the one described for shading (see pages 84-5).

SPRAYS

Sprays are of limited use in what is essentially a sharp-edged technique, and the results can look powdery and flat. They are also relatively expensive and not necessarily any quicker to use than paints. However, if you do choose to use a spray because it has a property you like, aim the jet horizontally and hold down the stencil very firmly so that the droplets do not seep underneath. For a solid coverage, sweep the spray back and forth over the area, allowing the surface to dry between applications. Avoid taking the spray too close to the surface or positioning the paint in one thick coat as it will run, leaving drizzly trails, and the surface may crack when dry.

MATERIALS AND EQUIPMENT

Stenciling brushes—sometimes called "pounce" brushes because of the up and down manner in which they are used—look rather like shaving brushes with the bristles chopped off square at the end. They come in several sizes with the smallest, used for very detailed stencils, called "fitches." These are round in section, flat-ended and very stiff. All these brushes are inexpensive, so there is no need to cut up other brushes to make substitutes.

Stenciling brushes leave a slightly grainy texture that resembles orange peel. If you want a smoother finish, try working instead with a sponge, folded rag, paint pad, or even an ordinary stiff artist's brush. However, if you use a conventional brush you will run the risk of smudging under the edge of the motif.

Other equipment you will need for stenciling includes a large saucer for each color of paint (never dip your brush straight into the can when stenciling), clean rags, solvent, masking tape, a level, pencil or chalk, and a plumbline or T-square for marking out the area to be stenciled.

MARKING OUT AN AREA

Before you start get down to work, it is important to mark out the positions of your stencils. If you are working on a wall, never take your measurements for verticals and horizontals from the walls and ceiling, because they are very rarely true. Instead, draw all the horizontal lines in pencil or chalk using a level, and take the verticals from these horizontals using a plumbline or T-square. Mark the position of each stencil on the wall in pencil through the holes in each corner.

To mark out a floor, first square it up by making a grid with chalk lines, and then indicate the position of each stencil as above. If you want a border, use chalk to mark out parallel lines around the main design, at equal distances from the walls all the way around. If you then discover that your supposedly square room is not square, and the corners are at 41° rather than 45° angles, draw your corner borders at about 43°.

A simple, symmetrical stencil design can be as striking as an elaborate one. A repeat motif of golden crowns on a neutral base color and the wooden paneling below give this room an almost medieval appearance.
(BELOW)

Take care to space out your stencils evenly to avoid a collision of motifs at the corners. Indicate the central point of each motif on the stencil itself and mark out these points between the lines.

APPLICATION

Fix the stencil into position with masking tape. Pour a little paint into a saucer and take a small amount onto the brush. Before you start stenciling, stamp the brush down firmly onto a paper towel to spread the paint evenly across the bristles and to get rid of any excess. Then, pressing the stencil firmly with your hand and working from the outside in, dab the thinly coated brush onto the stencil, rocking it very gently backwards and forwards to distribute the color evenly at each downward "pounce" of the brush. Avoid moving the brush sideways or you will risk getting paint under the stencil. When you have filled in the motif, allow the paint to dry for about 30 seconds. Now lift off the stencil, holding the bottom with one hand and gently peeling it back and up from the top. Transfer it to the next position. If the stencil board is going to overlap an adjacent one, apply the boards alternately to avoid smudging. If you are working in several colors, allow one color to dry before applying the next. As you work, paint will start to build up around the edges of the stencil. This should be cleaned off at intervals with a rag or sponge dipped in the appropriate solvent.

When you have finished, clean the stencils and brushes in the same solvent and store the stencils flat, separating them with aluminum foil or tissue paper. It is always worth hanging onto your stencils, because you may want to re-use the pattern or retouch the original work at a later date. Both oil-board and acetate stencils will last a lifetime if they are stored and looked after properly.

Once your stencilwork has dried, remove any chalk or pencil marks with a clean artist's eraser (putty rubber) as these may show up and sometimes even spread beneath the varnish. Leave water-based stenciling for one day and oil-based for two days before varnishing. For a hardwearing finish, protect stencilwork with two coats of matte or satin varnish. Stenciled floors will need at least three to five coats of varnish. Matte or satin varnish painted over a gloss varnish gives a soft sheen.

STENCILING FABRICS

The stiff fabric of many roller blinds is often ideal for stenciling. This is easiest to do when the material is laid flat. Hold the stencil firmly on the fabric and use a stiff, dry stencil brush to apply the fabric paint. Fix the design by ironing the reverse side of the fabric for at least two minutes, with the iron set according to the type of fabric.

A large-scale yet subtle stencil design applied over stippled walls. The inner curved edges of the stenciled leaves have been darkened slightly and the outer edges left deliberately blurred for a soft, hazy effect.
(ABOVE)

ANTIQUING

G iven time, colors fade and varnish takes on a yellowish tinge to produce the attractive patina of age. Many of the standard paint techniques can be used to give all kinds of surfaces and objects a mellow, time-worn look. Glazing, spattering and stippling can all be used on woodwork, colorwashing is best suited to walls and ceilings, and crackle glazes can be applied to virtually any surface to produce the effect known as "craquelure."

PAINT GLAZES ON WOOD
To achieve a convincing antiqued look you will need to consider how colors fade. As a rough guide, red fades to pink or dull orange, deep red fades to orange or brown; dark blue fades to gray, mid-blue to gray-green; light yellow fades to cream, deep yellow to amber; magnolia fades to cream, zinc white to gray and flake white to cream; and green fades to gray. The mottled and translucent appearance of aged paint can be evoked wonderfully through the use of oil glazes. Use a 3:1 mixture of paint to matte varnish, first adding a little oil glaze to the paint, to create a delicate finish with a high degree of transparency.

TINTED VARNISHES ON WOOD
You can use both tinted and untinted varnish over antiqued paint glazes. Although oil-based varnishes already have a yellowish tone, special colored antiquing varnishes can be used to exaggerate this tendency. To age moldings, apply an even coat of tinted glaze and then rub it off again with a cloth, leaving a little glaze in the crevices. Tinted

The stripped beams, distressed wooden cupboard doors and door frame, and patchy blue-gray and cream colorwash on the walls combine to give this bedroom a lived-in look.
(RIGHT)

and untinted glazes can also be used on the same surface to produce an uneven and worn-looking finish. For example, if you want to age a table-top, apply clear glaze in the center, and then brush tinted glaze into it from the sides, to emulate the darker

sometimes turns slightly gray with age. You can mimic this by using a trace of flake white or, for a more transparent effect, zinc white with a little lampblack. Use artist's oil pigments in oil-based glazes and either gouache or acrylic pigments in water-based paints. Use gray or brown tinted glazes to age a black surface.

NOTE: Flake-white oil pigment contains white lead and may be difficult to obtain. A flake white replacement is usually available at paint supply stores.

SPATTERING ON WOOD

Spattering can be used to simulate the fly-spots which freckle so much old painted or varnished woodwork. Oil-based paints, acrylics and brown or black ink are all highly effective. If you are using ink, coat the surface to be aged with varnish or shellac before spattering the surface, following the method on pages 88–9. Knowing where to spatter is the secret of success: the edges of drawers, and the tops and raised turnings of furniture legs and banisters, are the most convincing areas. Fly-spotting rarely occurs on flat surfaces, so restrict spattering here to the occasional line of dots, which should be slightly smudged.

CISSING

This is a technique in which spots of paint thinner are splashed onto wet oil-based paint, or water onto wet water-based paint, to produce a mottled, antique effect. Paint thinner can also be used on water-based paint and water on oil-based, for a slightly different effect. Both methods produce a very convincing aged appearance, which can be highlighted by finishing with a coat of tinted varnish. Gloss varnish usually looks out of place on an antiqued surface, so a soft satin sheen is generally more appropriate. Several coats of thinned, clear matte or satin varnish, even when applied over antiquing varnish, will give the best finish.

areas which appear around the edges of tables after years of wear.

The colors most frequently added to varnish when antiquing wood are the earth pigments: raw and burnt umber, raw and burnt sienna, and yellow ochre. White paint

Craquelure

CRAQUELURE ON WOOD

As oil-based paint ages it starts to crack, producing an irregular network of hair-line fractures. The same thing happens to varnish. This process is known as craquelure. Oil- and water-based crackle varnishes which simulate this aging effect can be obtained from art and specialist paint suppliers. Oil-based crackle varnishes are transparent and produce a convincing irregular cracking effect; however, they are more difficult to obtain and use than water-based versions. Crackle glazes are available in both transparent and opaque forms and, although they offer less variety of effect, they are more predictable in their behavior and easier to manipulate.

Crackle varnish, used only on those areas of the dresser that are subject to wear and tear, creates a convincing look of age.
(BELOW)

OIL-BASED CRACKLE VARNISHES

These are suitable for use on wood, painted canvas and board, but are not appropriate for walls. They are ideal for using over decorated or stenciled wood surfaces because they will not obscure the pattern. They may be harder to obtain than the water-based variety, but should be available from specialist trade suppliers or art supply stores.

Crackle varnishes are generally sold and used in a pair that consists of an antiquing varnish with a marked yellow tinge, and a separate crackle varnish. The former generally has a thick, molasses-like consistency and should be applied in an even layer with a stiff-bristled varnishing brush—a soft brush will shed hairs and fail to spread the varnish properly. The setting time varies, but you will usually need to wait about an hour before applying the crackle varnish on top. If no cracks have appeared within 45 minutes of applying the crackle varnish, use a hairdryer to blow warm air evenly over the surface. This will normally produce a pattern of fine cracks. Avoid holding the dryer too close or over one spot for too long: you will either melt the varnish, or create an intricate spiderweb which will look sensational for a minute, then vanish without trace.

Crackle varnishes sometimes fail to crack if the weather is humid or very cold. If both varnishes are applied in a cool place they may take several hours to crack. If, despite your efforts, the varnish still fails to crack, clean it off with water, unless specifically instructed otherwise, and start again. Alternatively, wait for the non-cracked crackle to dry, then paint on another coat of antiquing varnish followed by a second layer of crackle varnish. This may well crack successfully and you could get secondary cracks underneath.

WATER-BASED CRACKLE VARNISHES

Transparent water-based crackle varnishes work on the same principle as oil-based varieties, but they have much shorter drying and cracking times because they work by evaporation. Their main drawback is that they produce a crackle so regular that it is not entirely realistic.

TINTING CRACKLE VARNISH

Both oil- and water-based crackle varnishes are colorless, and although the fine fissures catch the light, adding a certain depth, the effect can be emphasized by tinting. Oil-based craquelure can be given a wash of 1:4 parts artist's oil pigment (preferably lampblack, burnt umber, or burnt sienna) to paint thinner. This should be wiped on with a lint-free rag and then polished off after a few moments with a second clean cloth, leaving a little of the stain in the cracks. Some manufacturers produce a lampblack tinting agent specifically for this purpose that is soluble in paint thinner. Water-based craquelure may be stained in the same way, using oil- or water-based paint; if you choose the latter you will need to work very fast, wiping it over a small area at a time. Another method is to tint one layer of craquelure and then to repeat the whole process, using a second layer of antiquing glaze and crackle glaze, and then tinting that too.

Most transparent crackle varnishes dry to a gloss or eggshell finish, but they benefit from having a matte or eggshell-matte clear varnish on top, as this enhances the tinted crackle and also evokes the softer surface of aged paint.

OPAQUE CRACKLE GLAZE

Another way to emulate the effect of old peeled and cracked paint on both walls and wood is to use crackle glaze. This is an opaque, water-based glaze that is applied between two layers of water-based paint; the subsequent chemical reaction causes the upper paint coat to fracture in scars to reveal the "old" color beneath, which can be very effective when contrasting colors are used. The process is very fast, as with all

acrylic-based paints. The glaze—the equivalent of the antiquing varnish in transparent craquelure—is laid over the dry base color, followed immediately by the top coat of paint, which shrinks on application before bursting to reveal the base coat. This craquelure generally fractures in a fretwork of crosses and long vertical or horizontal splits, as though the surface has been slashed with a knife.

Crackle glazes are not suitable for painting over a design as, being opaque, they will obliterate it, but they are excellent for use on doors and walls. The final effect is quite dramatic, so should not be used over-enthusiastically in an interior. It is generally best as a feature on walls or alcoves, or on doors or panels in conjunction with distressed walls. On a smaller scale, it can look very sophisticated on rubbed-down wooden objects and panels.

A delicate finish of fissures and fine lines can be created by applying oil-based crackle varnish over a cream base color. When the surface is dry, enhance the cracks with gray artist's oil color and protect with oil-based varnish. (LEFT)

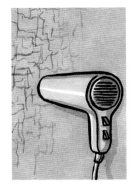

Apply a coat of crackle varnish over a layer of antiquing varnish with a stiff-bristled varnishing brush. (TOP)

If no cracks have appeared after 45 minutes or so, use a hairdryer to heat the surface gently. (ABOVE)

Aging wood and walls

Chipping dried paint from wood, tinting metal the color of verdigris, staining polished or varnished surfaces, and distressing plaster walls are just some of the ways in which to create the illusion of age.
(BELOW)

AGING WOOD WITH PAINT

To produce a worn, aged look on stripped and seasoned wood, apply oil-based paint directly to the surface without first priming it or using an undercoat. The paint will soak erratically into the most absorbent parts of the timber and lie near the surface on others, producing an authentically worn appearance. New wood can be stained—for example with gray oak woodstain—and then painted over in a similar manner and without using primer, so that the

paint soaks patchily into it, giving the appearance of old gray wood with a dusting of powdery paint.

A yellow wash applied with irregular brush-strokes over a strong green base color gives these walls a worn but lively appearance.
(RIGHT)

AGING WOOD BY REMOVING PAINT

One of the simplest ways to give paint finishes a worn appearance is to sand them lightly in patches. For a convincing effect, concentrate on those areas which would naturally receive the most wear and tear: for example, the edges and center of a table, and around the edges and handles of a cupboard or door. A disc sander will speed up the process and is ideal for use on large areas, but should never be used on delicate detailing.

DISTRESSING STENCILS AND PAINTED DESIGNS

Stencils and other painted decorations can be aged by sanding them, so that the whole design looks as though it has faded over many years. Fold the sandpaper around a tightly bunched cloth or a block of wood with rounded edges, and work with a firm, circular motion.

ANTIQUE COLORWASHING ON WALLS

To create a convincing look of age on walls, aim to add warmth to the existing color rather than making it darker. A gray wall can be warmed using a thin burnt umber wash and a pale blue one by using raw umber. Green walls need either a burnt umber or raw umber wash depending on how dark they already are, while white, off-white, yellow, beige and pink walls all benefit from a thin wash of burnt umber. Walls in older buildings tend to have curves and bumps in them so avoid any finish with a high gloss, which will only emphasize the undulations.

ANTIQUE SCUMBLE GLAZES ON WALLS

Oil-based glazes work very well on walls, bestowing a patina which is rarely achieved with a paint wash alone. The antiquing glaze tints are basically the same as those for antique colorwashing (see above), but do bear in mind that most oil-based glazes tend to have a yellow tone. If the colorwash is already yellow in tone, it is best to use a grayish glaze to avoid over-yellowing the color.

Tinted matte acrylic scumble glazes are ideal for use on uneven walls, as any tidemarks caused by the glaze drying out before it can be blended in will be less noticeable than on a completely smooth surface.

FAUX FINISHES

Marbling

Marble comes in an incredible variety of colors and its swirling patterns have long provided inspiration for all kinds of decorative effect. For centuries, master craftsmen and fine artists have produced painted marbles that are indistinguishable from the real thing. However, it is neither essential nor necessarily advisable to reproduce a specific type of marble in a domestic interior. The soft yellow and brown beauty of Sienna marble works superbly in small city apartments as well as in the libraries of large country houses, but the rococo extravagance of red and yellow Sicilian jasper would look somewhat alarming in the porch of a suburban bungalow. It is often best simply to convey the general effect, or essence, of marble, using whatever colors you decide look best.

Marbling works well on walls, floors, fireplaces, some windowsills, large solid furniture, and small decorative objects. However, it is generally advisable to avoid marbling anything which would never be made from stone. Whether you copy any of the wide number of real marbles or make up your own color mixtures, you should remember that almost all marbles have a strong sense of diagonal movement.

MATERIALS AND EQUIPMENT

It is possible to marble in both oil- and water-based paint, and even to mix the two, but the oil techniques are usually best over large areas. For oil marbling you will need flat oil paint, eggshell or undercoat, and a transparent oil-based glaze, artist's oil pigments, a small sea sponge, a soft 2–3in (50–75mm) paintbrush, a fine artist's brush, saucers, clean rags, newspapers, screw-topped jars, and paint thinner.

SIENNA MARBLE

Paint a pale yellow base color in flat oil paint, eggshell or undercoat. Mix yellow ochre pigment into an oil-based glaze and rag this over the base, or brush on using a loose swirling motion. Using a 2in (50mm) brush and raw sienna paint, add diagonal veins, blurring each one as soon as it has

These two marbled door panels are almost indistinguishable from the genuine stone. The cloudier finish of the lower panel was achieved by blending two or three different colors with loose, swirling brushstrokes; the detailed black-and-white design involved hand-painting veins with a small, fine brush after the mottled base colors had dried.
(RIGHT)

been applied by swirling another brush dipped in eggshell varnish through it. Smudge the glazed surface with crumpled newspaper, then soften the effect with a broad, dry brush to give a cloudy, mottled appearance. Using a fine artist's brush add a few more burnt umber veins and soften them very slightly. Finish by applying one or two coats of clear gloss varnish followed by one of satin varnish to give the surface an even eggshell sheen and greater depth.

Other marbling techniques

WATER-BASED MARBLING

It is possible to marble with water-based paint, but unless you are highly experienced the results tend to lack depth and possess the powdery, flat look of marbled wallpaper. If you are working with latex, apply the base color (the main color of the marble) and then brush the veins over it, softening them with a sponge or damp brush along either one or both sides simultaneously.

The most effective way to gain a sense of depth in this technique is to rag or ragroll the base color first. Do this by painting a pale wash over a slightly darker base, and then ragging the wash immediately after it is applied (see pages 90–1). The veins are then added over the top. Finish with clear satin varnish.

PAPER ROCKING

This is the paper counterpart of ragging and can be used with either oil- or water-based paints to produce a marbled effect. First paint a base coat of flat white latex or undercoat and leave to dry. Now add a contrasting layer of glaze tinted with artist's pigments or acrylics as appropriate. While it is still wet, press a rumpled and pleated sheet of thin paper against the glaze. The paper will gently raise, crease, and absorb the glaze, leaving a fretwork of

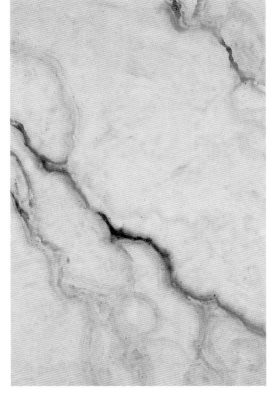

fine, irregular veins. If the creased paper is held against the surface and rubbed in places with a stiff brush, the shifting motion will merge the colors together and uncover other areas, to give an impression of depth and movement.

FLOATING COLOR

This is a method of marbling on a wet ground using oil-based paints diluted with paint thinner. First paint on a base color and allow it to dry. Brush on a coat of flatting oil—a mixture of 1:6 parts boiled linseed oil to paint thinner—followed by a very runny solution of the main color. Dab two or three other colors, all diluted to the same extent, onto the wet paint using a small brush. The colors should flow together easily. If the surface becomes too wet, dab it with a cotton ball dampened with paint thinner. Conversely, if the colors are not watery enough to flow, dab on a little extra paint thinner with a cotton ball.

For faux Sienna marble, rag an ochre oil-based glaze over a pale yellow base and leave to dry. Paint in the diagonal veins in raw sienna, blurring each immediately by swirling eggshell varnish across it. Soften the surface with crumpled newspaper and a broad, dry brush. (LEFT)

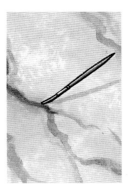

Apply the ochre glaze over the base color with a crumpled cloth, dabbing it on gently to create a mottled effect. (TOP)

Paint in the veins with a fine artist's brush, applying eggshell varnish simultaneously to soften and blur the lines. (ABOVE)

Add veining as described for Sienna marble. The only limitation of this method is that it must be executed on a horizontal surface.

Marbling floors

Floor paints, artist's oil pigments and wall paints are all suitable for marbling floors, although the last two need to be well protected with up to five coats of varnish. There is no point in marbling your floor if there are huge spaces between the floorboards: any attempt to paint the veins so that they "flow" over the gaps will destroy the illusion of stone. Nor is it wise to marble a floor in which the grain of the wood is particularly prominent, or one with obvious lumps where the boards join.

MARBLING WITH ARTIST'S OIL PIGMENTS AND WALL PAINTS

Provided the floor is level and any gaps are filled, the methods for floor painting are the same as those for other surfaces, using wall paints tinted to your chosen colors with artist's oil pigments. Because of the high level of wear on floors, you will need to use three coats of gloss or semi-gloss varnish topped with two matte coats. This gives depth and sheen to the surface as well as protecting it. Darker marbles and contrasting checker patterns of light and dark work especially well on floors. For the latter, work on an alternating grid system, painting one set of tiles first and, when those are dry, blocking off their edges with masking tape and painting in the remaining tiles.

MARBLING WITH FLOOR PAINT

Floor paints come in a limited color range but can be intermixed. Apply the base color at full strength, then add the veins using a mixture of 3:1 parts paint to paint thinner. Before this dries, add a little more of the base color between the veins to soften them, then blend the two wet edges together with a dry brush.

Trompe l'oeil and marbling combined to grand effect. The vertical column, diamond pattern and dado rail have been created with lining techniques, giving an effect of light and shade; the red faux marble wall by brushing a dark red glaze over a lighter red, then vigorously blending the two with broad, swirling brushstrokes.
(RIGHT)

Great stones

Portero black: A black marble with golden veins, often used for clocks or fireplaces. It looks spectacular under artificial lighting.

Breccia: The stunning Italian "cloud shadow" marble with gray, white, and purple puffs of color, or with brown and yellow mottling, looks good anywhere from baroque tombs to contemporary bathrooms.

Brocatello: A Spanish marble similar to red-and-yellow brocade. Its fine, delicate pattern looks highly effective on small objects or wall panels in moderate-sized rooms.

Carrara: The classic white marble, this is either a pure pearly white or appears with soft gray veins. It was widely used for statues, fireplaces, and mantlepieces.

Lapis lazuli: The original source of ultramarine-blue, this gorgeous stone is the deepest blue of the midsummer sky, shot through with golden flecks caused by iron pyrites.

Malachite: The brilliant emerald-green marble stained by natural copper, from Russia. In most interiors it is best used on smaller objects like knife handles and clocks.

Porphyry: Gray-green or purple-red with tiny white flecks, this is the marble beloved of the Pharaohs for statues of the gods (and themselves). Its deep texture makes it excellent for fireplaces, walls, baseboards, floors, tables, and any small solid object.

Rouge royale: A seductive pink marble with paler pink and soft white veins. It comes from southern France and resembles enormous pieces of expensive nougat.

Sienna: A soft golden yellow marble with brown veins and shadows that works equally well on both small and large scales.

Thessalian green: A dark spinach-green marble flecked with black and white, from Thessaly, Greece. This looks handsome on walls, objects, in small rooms—especially bathrooms—and in checker-patterned floors.

Woodgraining

A dark woodgraining effect evoking the appearance of walnut or mahogany marries well with a stylized white faux marble table-top. Neither finish is an exact replica of the genuine article, but the overall effect is subtle and understated.
(BELOW)

Like marbling, skilled woodgraining can be almost impossible to distinguish from the genuine article. However, on a simpler level it can be used to evoke the presence or essence of wood, without seeking to be an exact copy of a specific timber.

It may seem strange, but much graining is carried out over real wood. The reason for this is that nowadays, many doors, panels and baseboards are constructed from mixtures of timber that were never intended to be stripped bare, and which subsequently reveal unappealing colors or mixtures of textures. Graining allows you to control the patterns. It is precisely that attractive element in the grain which makes expensive woods expensive, and why graining is often used to emulate them.

Oil- or water-based paint, or a mixture of the two, can be used for graining, but natural stains such as vinegar are also suitable. What you must decide when carrying out woodgraining is whether you wish to portray a specific wood such as mahogany, bird's-eye maple, or oak, or aim for a more generalized wood effect.

MATERIALS AND EQUIPMENT
Professionals use a whole battery of specialist brushes for woodgraining and, although you can manage very well without most of them, a few are worth the investment if you wish to produce the most sophisticated results. These are a "flogger," used to beat the surface and create the texture of woodgrain; a "mottler," to produce mottled effects; a fine "writer" or "pencil liner," for painting in the ripples of the grain; and finally, the most versatile of all the brushes, a "badger softener," used, as its name suggests, to soften all the painted lines.

It is possible to make substitutes for some of the above brushes: a soft-bristled brush can be substituted for the mottler and badger softener, and a fine-pointed artist's brush can be used instead of a pencil liner. A graining brush can be made from a fine, stiff-bristled brush by cutting the bristles off square at the end and then cutting clumps out of it at irregular intervals to produce a semi-flexible comb. You can make a graining comb from notched plastic, linoleum or thin cardboard, and a notched cork is excellent for marking in knots. Other useful equipment includes a medium brush, a wallpaper brush, and artist's fitches, together with an artist's eraser, cotton swabs, a sponge, and clean rags.

Oil- and water-based graining

YELLOW PINE

Paint on an eggshell base coat of barley white and rub down with a little fuller's earth. Mix a pale brown water-based glaze using raw umber and raw sienna gouache colors. Thin these with a little water to give a transparent effect and apply the glaze with a broad, flat brush to create a texture of fine, undulating parallel lines. Soften with a badger softener and leave to dry.

Dilute a little raw umber and burnt sienna artist's oil pigments with paint thinner and add them to an oil-based glaze. Using a fine artist's brush, fill in the knots so that they slope downwards in long ovals. Soften them with a small badger softener and leave to dry. Using the same glaze, draw in the grain with either a flat fitch or a pencil liner. The grain should flow gently around the knots like water around pebbles, enclosing them in a series of long oval shapes ending with a long point downwards. Now, using a deeper version of this raw umber and burnt sienna glaze, strengthen the knots with an artist's brush. The outside rim of the knot should be darker than its center. Leave to dry for at least 24 hours.

Darken the lighter glaze with a small amount of lampblack artist's oil pigment thinned with paint thinner. Using a 1–2in (25–50mm) brush, apply this glaze quite unevenly over the whole surface, leaving a slightly grainy texture. Wipe out sections along the grain with an artist's eraser and soften them with a badger softener. When this is dry, seal the surface with a clear matte or satin varnish.

Oil-based graining

This is probably the most versatile of the graining techniques over large areas and can be achieved using an oil-based glaze tinted with artist's oil pigments, over an eggshell

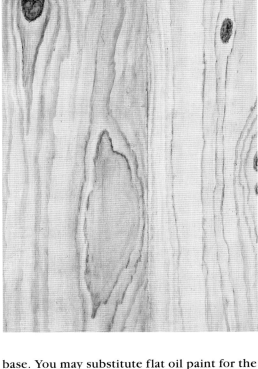

base. You may substitute flat oil paint for the base color, but it will need a coat of shellac or satin varnish before you start graining to allow the glazes to flow easily.

EUROPEAN ASH

Brush on a base coat of creamy beige eggshell and allow to dry for at least 24 hours. Next, wipe a thin layer of transparent oil-based glaze over the surface with a lint-free cloth. Now tint some more glaze with a mixture of artist's oil pigments in raw umber, raw sienna and a trace of lampblack, diluting them first in a little paint thinner. Using a small, flat brush—a bristle "fitch" is ideal—use the tinted glaze to paint the grain. This should flow downwards in gentle, shallow curves, with a slight wobble every inch or so. Soften the inside edge of the grain with a badger softener or a soft, dry brush. Leave to dry for at least 24 hours.

To reproduce the effect of stripped yellow pine, brush a pale brown water-based glaze over a barley-white base. When this has dried, paint in the knots using a dark brown oil-based glaze. Leave to dry again before adding the lines of the woodgrain. (LEFT)

Paint in the knots before you apply the grain. They should be slightly darker on the outside than in the center. (BELOW)

Draw in the grain with a fine artist's brush. The lines should flow around the knots like water flowing around pebbles. (BOTTOM)

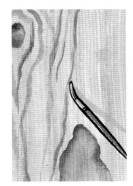

Many very early examples of graining and marbling were more symbolic than realistic. This highly stylized woodgraining effect flaunts its artificiality. (RIGHT)

Now tint a darker transparent oil-based glaze using the same pigments as before. Apply the glaze evenly with a 1in (25mm) brush, leaving slight variations in the tone. Using an artist's eraser or a dry rag, wipe off small areas of the glaze to leave well-spaced, diagonal patches about 3–4in (75–100mm) long, tilting the shapes at slightly different angles. Soften these by striking them lightly with a badger softener.

While the glaze is still wet, lighten the inner edges of the grain using a cotton swab. Lastly, using a dry flogger, beat the surface lightly to give it a fine, fibrous texture. After leaving this to dry for 24 hours, seal it with two coats of clear mid-satin or eggshell varnish.

MAHOGANY

Apply an eggshell base coat of orange-salmon and leave it to dry for at least 24 hours. Tint some transparent oil glaze in several shades using artist's pigments in burnt umber and lampblack, first diluting them in a little paint thinner.

Using a 1in (25mm) brush, brush a medium-dark glaze upwards in a series of sweeping arcs first from one side, then the other, so that the arcs join at the top. Allow the lighter base color to show through on the upward sweep and make the join the darkest part. Now, using a darker glaze of the same color, strengthen some of the ribs and stipple the center so that it is noticeably darker along the spine. Using a flat wallpaper brush, brush over the rib pattern to strengthen it, flicking downwards just as you come to the edge of the spine. Then soften the whole surface with a badger softener, striking at right-angles to the rib pattern.

If you want a swirling movement in the woodgrain, move a brush over the ground coat in a series of strong, diagonal arcs from the base of the surface you are decorating.

Using a wallpaper brush, sweep over the swirls roughly and then soften the whole area with a badger softener, leaving some areas sharper than others.

When graining vertically, for example down the side panels of a door, employ the same method but use a brush in a series of soft, wavering verticals, before softening the whole effect with a series of downward diagonals. Most Victorian mahogany was finished to a very high gloss, but you may prefer to use a coat of satin varnish.

EBONY

This black hardwood is often used as a molding on cupboard panels. First apply a ground of gesso (see page 201 for recipe) or up to three coats of artist's acrylic primer. Once this is dry, rub it down using fine sandpaper. Mix equal amounts of artist's acrylic pigments in lampblack and burnt umber, and paint this evenly over the surface using an artist's brush. When dry, finish with two coats of acrylic eggshell varnish.

USING COMBS AND ROCKERS

The wavy grain of softwoods such as pine can be emulated by running a comb through wet glaze. Brush an oil, acrylic or a paint glaze freely over a base color, then run a wide or narrow comb, either wrapped in a clean cloth or uncovered, through the glaze to remove it in wavering parallel lines. The effect can be softened by crossing the lines diagonally with a dry brush. Finer grains can be added with an artist's brush or a pencil liner over small areas that have first been wiped clean with a cloth. Also available are rubber "rockers" that work on the same principle as ink stamps. These are loaded with paint and then dragged over a surface and gently rocked at different angles to produce a naturalistic graining effect.

Tortoiseshelling

The use of real and simulated tortoiseshell originated in the Far East, where it was commonly presented in exquisite panels mounted in ivory and ebony and incorporated into lacquered boxes and small luxury items. Tortoiseshell first became popular in Europe in the seventeenth century and cabinetmakers were quick to replicate its distinctive patterning on furniture, cornices, and ceilings, where it appeared as inset oval or circular panels.

The natural coloring of tortoiseshell ranges from golden honey to tawny auburn to an almost fiery red. However, like marbling, its name has become synonymous with its characteristic markings, and this can be reproduced in any combination of colors, whether deep chestnut over emerald, or burnt sienna over deep blue.

Tortoiseshelling can be carried out using oil- or water-based paints and varnishes. Oil-based paints are easier to use for large, vertical panels, water-based for smaller, horizontal ones.

WHERE TO USE TORTOISESHELL

A tortoiseshell finish is undeniably handsome but can look overwhelming if used over a large area. If you decide to use tortoiseshell on a wall, it is best to divide up the area into panels no larger than 3ft (90cm) square. Create the panels separately so that each one has its own identity. Use chalk or pencil to mark them out, then attach masking tape along the edges of each area. Complete the tortoiseshell panels before painting the areas between them, using masking tape along the edges to keep each area separate.

Tortoiseshelling works well on doors but, as with walls, restrict yourself to smaller areas and tortoiseshell only the panels rather than carrying the effect across the whole surface. Paint the surrounding wood in an ivory color or to emulate ebony (see page 115).

Oil-based tortoiseshelling

GOLDEN TORTOISESHELL

First apply a base coat of light oil-based eggshell paint in sandy yellow or rich cream. Tortoiseshell has a radiating movement, so that color bands appear almost to diverge. To recreate this look, apply light or dark oak varnish with a flat, stiff-bristled varnishing brush, working diagonally across the area from one top corner downwards. If you are painting on a wall, unthinned light

An exuberant oil-glazed tortoiseshell pattern decorates a bath and door. The design has been well executed, with the mottling pattern kept small and even.
(BELOW)

oak varnish will flow best. On wood, use thinned light or dark oak varnish. Before it sets, brush the varnish into a series of zig-zag bands of varying widths. Using cotton or a rag soaked in paint thinner, soften the edges of these varnish bands so that they can receive paint. With an artist's brush about ½in (12mm) wide, stroke in raw umber artist's oil pigment, diluted 1:1 with paint thinner, using a zig-zag motion. Apply a little burnt umber oil pigment, similarly diluted, into the middle of the raw umber areas. When you have done this, soften the edges into the varnish by stroking the whole surface lightly with a dry brush, working alternately in the direction of the dark patterns and at right-angles to them. Keep going until you are happy with the results. If you are working on a horizontal surface you can add texture to the surface by splashing on a few drops of paint thinner from an eye dropper or by spattering it very lightly across the surface (see Cissing, page 103).

Water-based tortoiseshelling

AUBURN TORTOISESHELL

Although traditionally a lacquer-based technique, tortoiseshelling can also be carried out using water-based paints, albeit on the smallest scale. On a gesso ground (see page 201 for recipe) paint on a light terracotta base color consisting of 2 parts light red, 2 parts burnt umber, 1 part titanium white and 1 part yellow ochre (or yellow oxide) artist's acrylics mixed into white latex. Then mix 1 part light red and 1 part burnt umber in an acrylic glaze and coat the terracotta evenly, simultaneously dabbing a little ivory black into the glaze to create a mottled effect. Cross this with a dry brush so that the ivory black merges into the glaze and leave to dry. If you wish, you can add a second acrylic glaze containing a small amount of cadmium yellow.

FINISHES
In addition to the examples given here, any other color combination can be used in either medium to create a tortoiseshell effect. Oil-based work does not need varnishing unless you want a particularly high gloss finish, but if you have used water-based paints your work will need more protection. Never use a matte varnish on tortoiseshell. It will kill the color and depth by obliterating the light-reflecting qualities of the varnishes beneath. A satin varnish is more suitable.

For the most sophisticated and realistic finish, apply a coat of semi-gloss polyurethane and sand it down with a very fine wet-and-dry paper, using a solution of water and mild soap flakes. Then mix a solution of rotten-stone (powdered decomposed limestone available from artist's suppliers and hardware stores) and warm linseed oil to a paste and use it to polish the surface.

Brush an oil-based varnish tinted with burnt sienna evenly over a sand yellow base color. While this is still wet, add smudges of varnish and burnt umber and black oil paints, then blend with criss-cross, diagonal strokes from a dry brush. (LEFT)

Dab patches of black and burnt umber oil paint simultaneously into a wet burnt sienna oil glaze. (TOP)

Blend the patches with criss-cross strokes from a broad, dry softening brush to produce the characteristic mottled finish of tortoiseshell. (ABOVE)

Trompe l'oeil

Trompe l'oeil is an art rather than a craft, in which the illusion of a three-dimensional form is created on a flat surface. Although the most sophisticated effects need a high degree of skill, it is nonetheless possible for an imaginative amateur to produce some surprisingly attractive results with the judicious use of basic observation, lining, shading, and collage.

You can place a trompe effect anywhere provided that the structure of the surface on which it will be painted does not disrupt the design. You should also bear in mind the fall of natural light in the area. An area which receives little direct light, such as a shaded room, is ideal; however, if there is direct light, paint the trompe as though the light were facing directly onto it or just a little to one side. For example, in a trompe alcove with shelves, paint the rear of the alcove a tone darker than that of the surrounding walls, and both the illusory inside sides of the alcove two tones darker, with the front of the shelves very pale.

It is equally important to consider the ways in which the site of your trompe l'oeil is artificially lit. If you paint a highlight which will be in shadow once the artificial light is on, or vice versa, the illusion may be spoiled. Try either to light the area so that the light falls evenly onto the surface, or angle the beams to enhance the effect.

For the basic principles of trompe l'oeil shading, see the Empire-style Salon project on pages 142-5.

A very sophisticated trompe l'oeil which plays upon the differences between art and reality. The swagged drapery looks three-dimensional, but is used to frame a picture which has been painted to appear deliberately flat and stylized. The "marbled" floor, so obviously wooden, is another piece of visual trickery.
(LEFT)

PAINT
The surface should be prepared according to the type of paint you will be using. Decorating paints are quite adequate for the base colors of wall areas, but the actual trompe itself should be carried out in artist's oil pigments or artist's acrylics.

FINISHING
A trompe l'oeil should always be finished in matte varnish, ideally an acrylic rather than an oil-based one. A gloss finish will destroy the illusion instantly by catching the light where there is supposed to be deep shade.

A trompe l'oeil in the colors and style of a Roman mural. Genuine undulations in the plaster have been incorporated into the design, making the illusory stonework of the dado even more convincing.
(BELOW)

THE BASIC METHODS DESCRIBED IN THE
TECHNIQUES AND EFFECTS CHAPTER ARE HERE
TAKEN A STEP FURTHER WITH A SERIES OF IMAGINATIVE
AND INNOVATIVE ROOM SCHEMES FROM THE TALENTED
BRUSH OF DAVID CARTER.

projects

*DAVID CARTER HAS CREATED a series of new projects
that incorporate many of the paint decoration techniques
described elsewhere in the book. His flamboyant,
theatrical room treatments are based on a
combination of broken-color effects such as
colorwashing and stenciling; antiquing
effects, including the use of crackle glaze;
and faux effects such as woodgraining and
trompe l'oeil. Most of the projects—from a
Klimt-inspired bathmat to a fake fur wall—
form part of a whole room scheme, but each
element can be used individually, combined
with other projects, or used alongside your
own ideas, to create a finished design
that is both stunning and unique. In the
following pages, clear instructions are accompanied by
inspiring photographs and explanatory illustrations
to clarify the specifics of each paint technique. The
sensational results speak for themselves.*

The enigmatic silhouetted figures painted on the walls of this
elegant French salon evoke an atmosphere of intrigue and mystery.
To achieve this effect yourself, turn to the project on pages 152–3.

CRACKLE-GLAZED HEADBOARD

The wonderfully mellow and "antiqued" appearance of this headboard—perfect for the tranquil ambience of a bedroom—was created using the highly effective technique of crackle glaze. The thick, water-based glaze was applied between two layers of latex paint, causing the top layer to crack and split: this left small areas of the off-white base coat visible, and produced the characteristic cracked effect of aged paintwork.

A wooden surface, such as that used here, makes the ideal foundation for any antiquing or distressing effect, especially those involving the use of crackle glazes and crackle varnishes, but any other correctly primed surface can also be used (see pages 194–8). In this instance, the crackle-glazed headboard was treated to frame a delicate and beautiful "Wings of Desire" stencil.

Headboard

Materials
Latex brush
Off-white and dull
  green flat
  latex paint
Containers for mixing
Medium, soft brush
Acrylic crackle glaze
Hairdryer
Raw umber artist's
  acrylic
Acrylic scumble glaze
Sea sponge
Satin finish acrylic
  varnish
Varnish brush

Before applying any paint, ensure that the prepared surface is completely clean and dry. Using the latex brush, apply a solid, even base coat of off-white latex, and leave to dry for 2–4 hours. Prepare the green latex to be used for the top coat by diluting it with water until you get a flowing, creamy consistency.

1 Once the green base coat has dried, use the medium brush to apply an even coat of acrylic crackle glaze over the base coat, working quickly so as not to leave any brushmarks. Adjust the thickness of the glaze depending on the result required: the thicker the glaze, the bolder the final cracking effect will be. Altering the direction of the brushstrokes will help to promote random cracking; working in one direction will create a more uniform result.

3 Using a clean brush, apply the top coat of diluted green latex. As with the glaze, control the direction of the cracking by altering the direction of your brushstrokes. The water in the paint will instantly activate the dried glaze, and the paint will split and shrink to produce the cracking. The cracking continues as the top coat dries: use the hairdryer to accelerate the process if you wish (this will also produce more dramatic splits in the paint), or leave overnight.

4 Once you are sure that the paint has dried out thoroughly, mix the raw umber artist's acrylic with some acrylic scumble glaze and a little water, and lightly sponge this wash onto the paintwork to soften the effect and give an antique look to the cracking. A sea sponge is best for this (see page 86). Leave to dry for 1–2 hours. To seal and protect the head-board, apply 2 even coats of satin finish acrylic varnish, allow-ing the first coat to dry for 2 hours before applying the second.

heat the surface using a hairdryer on a low setting. Hold the dryer at least 12in (30cm) away, and move it continually to avoid overheating the surface. If you want to speed up the drying process even further, you can try applying the heat immediately after painting on the glaze. However, you may not achieve such an effective result this way.

2 Leave the glaze to dry for 2 hours. Then, to evaporate any remaining moisture thoroughly, gently

KLIMT-INSPIRED BATHROOM

The walls of this plain but wonderfully light and sunny bathroom have been "lifted" by the addition of flowing, branch-like spirals. The neutral base color was created with a glaze to give the look of an old plaster finish, and the swirls and borders were painted a "dirty" orange, then brushed over with a lemon gold powder and acrylic scumble mix to add a subtle glow. The "bathmat" design was painted over a warm terracotta base color to tone with the walls. The blue borders and "watery" details were then added, and a gold fringe stenciled at either end.

Swirled walls

Using the latex brush, apply 2 coats of white latex over the walls, allowing each coat to dry for 2–4 hours. Mix a glaze from 2 parts warm-pink latex, 7 parts acrylic scumble and 1 part water, adding touches of burnt umber and burnt sienna artist's acrylics to "deaden" the color a little (see page 83 for more about mixing glazes). Using the soft, wide brush or acrylic glazing brush, apply the glaze to the walls, brushing in long, sweeping strokes to create a feeling of movement. There should be subtle transitions where the glaze has been applied more heavily in one area than in another. Leave to dry for 24 hours, then apply a second coat of glaze and leave to dry once again. For greater depth, and a gently "antiqued" appearance, add a little more pink latex to the remaining glaze, then apply this randomly over the walls. Use a dry softening brush to soften out the edges and create "blushes" of color. Allow to dry for 2 hours.

Materials
Latex brush
White and warm-pink satin latex paint
Acrylic scumble glaze
Burnt umber, burnt sienna, raw umber and raw sienna artist's acrylics
Containers for mixing
Soft, wide brush or acrylic glazing brush
Softening brush
Tracing paper
Pencil
Stiff cardboard
Stencil-cutting materials (see page 98)
Low-tack masking tape
Orange vinyl silk latex paint
2 x flat 1in (2.5cm) artist's brushes
Lemon gold powder or gold acrylic paint
Clean cloth

1 On tracing paper, draw 3 swirl stencils in varying sizes. Do this freehand, as the irregularities will disguise the fact that stencils have been used, and will create a more pleasing and painterly effect. Transfer the drawings to stiff cardboard, and cut out (see pages 98–9).

2 There is no particular method in the plotting of the swirls. It is a good idea to start with the largest ones, as these will provide a "framework," but having done these it is simply a question of judging their positions by eye. Use low-tack masking tape to attach each stencil to the wall, then outline the swirls faintly in pencil.

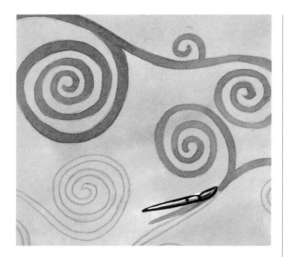

3 Having drawn in a reasonable number of swirls, draw in some of the connecting lines. Mix up a "dirty" orange color, using an off-the-shelf orange latex diluted 3:1 with water, and tinted with a little raw umber and raw sienna artist's acrylics to achieve the desired tone. Using a flat artist's brush, fill in the outlined swirls and lines: as with cutting the stencils, any irregularity here will contribute to the effect. Leave to dry for 1–2 hours. Mix lemon gold powder into acrylic scumble (or use gold acrylic paint), and paint this over the dirty orange, using another flat artist's brush. Do not apply the gold too solidly or evenly: keep the brush fairly dry, and wipe the color back in places with a cloth to give a softly "aged" effect.

Floor and bathmat

Prepare the floor surface for painting, as appropriate (see pages 194–8). Here, the floor consisted of plain wooden floorboards. Using the latex brush, apply 2 coats of white latex, allowing each coat to dry for 2–4 hours. Because heat rises, floors are generally colder than other surfaces in a room as well as being more prone to draughts, and depending on the weather, you may well find that you need to allow extra time for paints to dry.

Decide on the position and size of the "bathmat," draw the outline using a triangle and pencil, and apply low-tack masking tape inside this edge. Mix a glaze from 2 parts turquoise latex, 7 parts acrylic scumble and 1 part water. Using the wide brush or acrylic glazing brush, apply the glaze to the floor around the masked-off area, covering small sections at a time and quickly using the dragging brush to drag the glaze in one direction before it dries (see pages 92–3). Allow to dry for 24 hours, then repeat, this time dragging across the first coat to achieve a cross-dragged effect. Leave to dry, then remove the tape.

Materials
Latex brush
White satin latex
  paint
Triangle
Pencil
Low-tack masking
  tape
Turquoise satin latex
  paint
Acrylic scumble glaze
Soft, wide brush or
  acrylic glazing
  brush
Dragging brush
Warm-pink satin latex
  paint
Venetian red and
  burnt umber artist's
  acrylics
Softening brush
Tracing paper
Carbon or transfer
  paper
Medium artist's brush
Dark blue latex
3 fine artist's brushes
Lemon gold powder
  or gold acrylic paint
White and mid-blue
  artist's acrylics
Oiled stencil board or
  clear acetate
Stencil-cutting
  materials (see
  page 98)
Saucer
Stencil brush
Paper towels
Satin oil-based
  varnish
Varnish brush

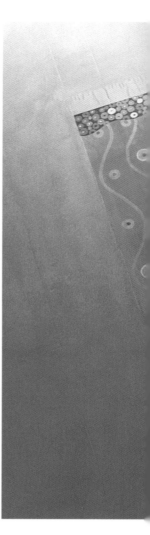

1 Re-apply masking tape on the outer edges of the unpainted bathmat area. Mix a glaze from 2 parts warm-pink latex, 7 parts acrylic scumble and 1 part water, and add touches of Venetian red and burnt umber artist's acrylics. Using a wide brush or acrylic glazing brush, apply this glaze to the bathmat area, immediately softening the glaze with a dry softening brush as you work. Leave to dry for 24 hours, then

3 Using the medium artist's brush and dark blue latex, paint in the wavy borders at either end of the mat, and leave to dry for 2–4 hours. Mix lemon gold powder with acrylic scumble (or use gold acrylic paint). Using a fine artist's brush and the gold paint, paint in the wavy lines, and then the "bubbles" on the central area and blue borders of the mat. Then paint in the white and blue "bubbles," using artist's acrylics diluted with a little water. Leave to dry for 2 hours. Make a very simple stencil for the fringes from oiled stencil board or acetate, and cut out (see page 98). Using masking tape to secure the stencil, pour a little gold paint into a saucer, and stencil in one fringe (see page 101). Repeat at the other end of the mat, then leave to dry overnight. Finally, apply 4 coats of satin varnish over the whole floor, allowing each coat to dry for 16 hours.

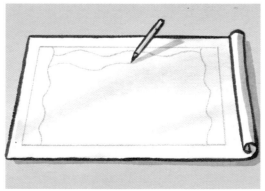

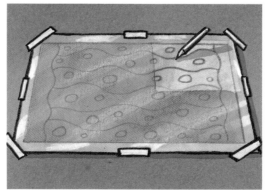

remove the masking tape. Draw out the design for the mat onto tracing paper but do not attempt to make the "bubbles" too perfect, as the irregularity of their size and shape is integral to the charm of the finished design.

2 Place the tracing paper over the mat area on the floor, and hold it in position with several lengths of masking tape. Slip a sheet of carbon or transfer paper beneath the tracing paper and then draw over the pattern, section by section, to transfer it to the floor.

DAMASK BEDROOM

Old and new have been successfully combined on these bedroom walls to emulate the richness of time-worn damask. An off-the-shelf latex paint in shocking pink was mixed as a glaze for the ground color, and the same latex base, used full strength and "dirtied" by adding a touch of burnt umber artist's acrylic, was used for the stencil color. The repeat pattern was stenciled over the walls, and then simply rubbed back to produce the authentically faded quality. A ceiling painted in the same ground color, and a "baseboard" in the deeper shade, completes the effect.

1 Fix the large stencil on the wall (in the first marked position), using low-tack masking tape. Pour a little of the stenciling color into a saucer, and dip the tip of the stencil brush vertically into it to coat the ends of the bristles evenly. Be careful not to overload the brush.

Materials
Latex brush
White and shocking-pink satin latex paint
Acrylic scumble glaze
Containers for mixing
Soft, wide brush or acrylic glazing brush
Pencil
Level
Plumbline or T-square
Oiled stencil board or clear acetate
Stencil-cutting materials (see page 98)
Burnt umber artist's acrylic
Low-tack masking tape
Saucer
Stencil brush
Paper towels
Rag
Scouring pad

Stenciled walls

Using the latex brush, apply 2 base coats of white satin latex paint to the walls and ceiling, allowing each coat to dry for 2–4 hours. Prepare the glaze for the ground color by mixing 2 parts shocking-pink latex paint, 7 parts acrylic scumble glaze and 1 part water (see page 83 for more about mixing glazes). Using a wide brush or acrylic glazing brush, apply the glaze evenly and briskly. Leave this to dry for 24 hours, then add a second coat of glaze to build up a rich color. When this is dry, grid up each wall (see page 131) to plot the positions of the large stencils, marking the positions lightly in pencil. (The two small motifs are added in afterwards.) Draw and then cut out the stencils (see page 98). Mix some undiluted pink latex paint with a touch of burnt umber artist's acrylic to make the stenciling color.

2 Dab the brush firmly on a "test" surface of paper towels to remove excess paint and distribute the remainder evenly across the bristles. There should not be any moisture visible on the brush.

3 Dab paint into the motif area, holding the brush at right-angles to the wall and using a light, pouncing action. You may need to use one hand to keep the stencil pressed firmly against the wall. Reload the brush as necessary.

4 When the motif is complete, leave the stencil for 30 seconds before removing the masking tape. Lift off the stencil, holding the bottom with one hand and gently peeling it away from the top. Place the stencil in the next marked position and repeat the process to fill all the motifs. At intervals, wipe away any paint that has built up on the stencil, using a rag dipped in water. Stencil the small motifs below the larger ones, positioning them by eye. Leave to dry overnight. Dampen the scouring pad slightly,

and use this gently in a circular motion to rub over the stenciled pattern. Run masking tape around the wall, about 6in (15cm) from the floor, and use the latex brush and remaining stenciling color to paint in the baseboard area. When dry, remove the tape.

OPULENT HALLWAY

O pulent faux effects on a starburst wall and mosaic floor unite here to create a decor of unparalleled elegance. The luxurious texture of button-backed upholstery was the inspiration behind the wall scheme, the rich royal purple punctuated with stenciled "creases" and "buttons." The effect is complemented perfectly by the natural tones of the faux mosaic floor, whose illusion was created by photocopying and transferring the design, adding a touch of color with a purple glaze, and painting a "shadow" line to produce the trompe l'oeil outline. An over-glaze, "dirtied" with raw umber and brushed over the entire floor, produced the softly antiqued appearance.

Starburst wall

Using the latex brush, apply 2 coats of white latex paint, allowing each coat to dry for 2–4 hours. Mix a glaze from 2 parts purple latex, 7 parts acrylic scumble and 1 part water (see page 83 for more about mixing glazes). Use a wide brush or acrylic glazing brush to apply this over the white base, working into it with a rag or dry softening brush as you go to create a slightly textured appearance. Leave the textured glaze to dry for 24 hours, and then repeat the process.

Materials
Latex brush
White and deep-purple
  satin latex paint
Acrylic scumble glaze
Container for mixing
Soft, wide brush or
  acrylic glazing brush
Clean rags
Softening brush
Steel measuring tape
Pencil
Wooden batten
Level
Plumbline or T-square
Length of thread or
  string
Low-tack masking
  tape
Oiled stencil board
  or clear acetate
Stencil-cutting
  materials (see
  page 98)
Gold acrylic paint
Burnt umber artist's
  acrylic
Saucer
Stencil brush
Paper towels

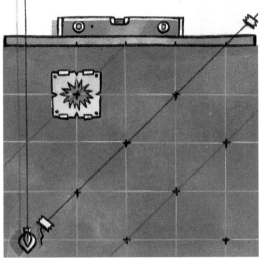

1 Work out a grid for each wall: the gap between the motifs should be approximately 12in (30cm). Measure out this spacing across and down the wall (a sectioned-off batten will be helpful for this). Use a level to check the horizontals, and a plumbline or T-square to check the verticals, and draw the grid lightly in pencil. Now double-check that every pattern is aligned correctly: this can be done by using a length of thread or string taped to the wall with low-tack masking tape, as shown.

2 Draw the designs for the "crease" and the "button" freehand on paper: the "button" should be approximately 1in (2.5cm) in diameter, and the "crease" should measure approximately 5in (13cm) between the 2 longest points. Transfer the designs to the oiled stencil board or acetate, and cut out each of them carefully (see page 98).

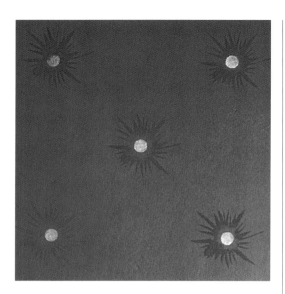

Faux mosaic floor

Prepare the floor surface for painting, as appropriate (see pages 194–8). Using the latex brush, paint the floor with 2 base coats of off-white flat latex paint, allowing each coat to dry for 2–4 hours. For the colored pieces of "mosaic," prepare a small quantity of glaze, using 2 parts purple latex, 7 parts acrylic scumble and 1 part water (see page 83 for more about mixing glazes). Separate the glaze into 2 containers. Dilute one of the quantities 3:1 with water, then add a small amount of raw umber artist's acrylic (this will be used for the trompe l'oeil shadows).

Materials

Latex brush
Off-white flat latex paint
Deep-purple satin latex paint
Acrylic scumble glaze
Containers for mixing
Raw umber artist's acrylic
3 large sheets of paper
Pencil

Black felt-tipped pen
Steel measuring tape
Paper towels
Saucer
Printer's blanket wash
Low-tack masking tape
Small artist's brush
Fine artist's brush
Soft, wide brush
Softening brush
Satin oil-based varnish

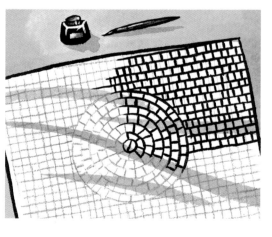

 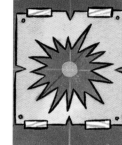

3 Place the "crease" stencil on top of the "button" one, with the button centered in the crease, and trim to the same size. To help position the stencils correctly, make small holes at each corner and cut V-shaped notches (or draw short lines if using acetate) at the center of each edge so that they can be placed accurately on the grid lines. Attach the "button" stencil to the wall in the first marked position, and stencil (see page 101) with gold acrylic paint. Fill in the "buttons," using a damp rag to remove paint build-up on the stencil at intervals.

4 Tint some purple latex with a little burnt umber artist's acrylic paint and repeat the process with the "crease" stencil. Take care to dab the paint only into the creases, leaving an unpainted area around the "button" so that it appears to float. Turn the stencil occasionally, still lining it up on the grid, to vary the direction of the points and imitate the appearance of upholstered fabric.

1 On three large sheets of paper, draw out the three separate "components" of the mosaic design in pencil: a corner square with circles inside it, an interlocking border motif, and a plain area of

"mosaic." When you are happy with the designs, draw over the outlines again using a black felt-tipped pen. Measure the floor area to estimate how many pieces of each design component you will need, then photocopy each sheet as many times as you require.

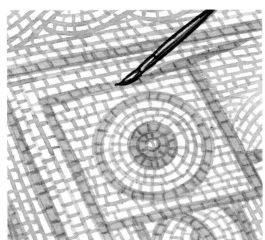

3 Repeat the process over the entire floor surface, starting by filling in the corner squares, following this with the borders and finally the plain areas. Leave to dry overnight. Carefully paint in the colored areas to frame each element, using the prepared purple glaze and the small artist's brush.

5 Mix a "dirty" over-glaze from acrylic scumble, water and a little raw umber artist's acrylic, and use the wide brush to apply this over the floor surface. Wipe back the glaze in places then soften it lightly with a dry softening brush. Allow to dry for 24 hours. Finally, apply 4 protective coats of satin varnish, leaving each coat to dry for 16 hours before applying the next.

4 To give the treatment greater depth, use the prepared trompe l'oeil mixture and a fine artist's brush, adding thin, freehand shadow lines to pick out the "mosaic" squares.

2 Dampen a tightly folded paper towel in a saucer of blanket wash. Beginning with a corner square, tape the first photo-copy inkside-down on the floor, and wipe the reverse side lightly with the paper towel to loosen the ink on the photocopy. Dampen the kitchen paper again, and this time wipe over the reverse of the photo-copy, applying a firm and constant pres-sure. Leave for 2 minutes, then carefully peel back one corner of the paper to check that the image has been transferred. If it is still faint, wipe over it again. Peel off the paper completely.

THE WRITING ON THE WALL

Stylized lettering on a warm red-on-pink ground color adds a touch of French sophistication and humor to what might otherwise be rather austere surroundings. The glowing wall tone was achieved by painting two coats of an oil-based red glaze over a pink base color; this glaze was then softened with a clean, dry brush almost immediately after application. The outlines for the lettering were applied using a simple transfer method, before being filled in using a fine artist's brush and gold oil-based paint.

Wall lettering

Using the 3½in (9cm) brush, apply a coat of warm-pink eggshell to the walls. Leave to dry for 24 hours, then repeat to create a good, even base coat. Mix a glaze from oil-based glaze combined with artist's oil colors, or other tinting medium, which you have mixed previously with a little paint thinner: cadmium deep red with a little raw and burnt sienna will produce a suitable tint (see page 82 for more about mixing glazes). Use the same brush to apply this glaze over the pink base, brushing it out in all directions and softening the glaze as you work using a brush or rag. Allow the glaze to dry for 24 hours, then brush on a second coat to create a rich sheen of color.

Materials
Soft 3½in (9cm)
  brush
Warm-pink eggshell
  paint
Container for mixing
Oil-based glaze
Artist's oil colors e.g.
  cadmium deep red,
  raw and burnt
  sienna or other
  tinting media
Paint thinner
Clean rag
Pencil
Tracing paper
Level
T-square
Carbon or transfer
  paper
Low-tack masking
  tape
Gold oil-based paint
Fine artist's brush

1 Look in books or magazines to find suitable lettering, then enlarge each letter using a photocopier. Draw the outline of each letter on to individual sheets of tracing paper.

2 Decide on the positioning of the letters. Using the level, lightly draw a horizontal base line in pencil. Work out the spacing, and use the T-square to draw in vertical guidelines so that the letters will be upright. With a sheet of carbon or transfer paper underneath, attach the first sheet of tracing paper to the wall with low-tack masking tape. Draw around the outline in pencil. Remove the papers, and you will find the letter transferred to the wall. Repeat with each letter. Using the fine artist's brush and gold oil-based paint, fill in the outlines.

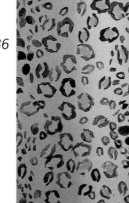

FAUX FUR INTERIOR

The wildness of the animal kingdom is brought indoors with this eye-catching design. The printing was carried out using the quick and easy medium of cut potatoes: their rough outlines contributed to the naturalistic effect, which is also enhanced by the background stripes in natural shades of taupe and cream. These stripes were painted first, and the prints, in ivory black artist's acrylic, were then added randomly over the surface. You may find it useful to refer to a photograph of a real animal skin while printing, although, as this is a fun treatment rather than a serious faux finish, working by eye alone will be equally successful.

Leopard-print wall

Materials
Latex brush
White vinyl flat latex
   paint
Taupe and cream flat
   latex paint (optional)
Raw sienna and yellow
   ochre artist's
   acrylics
Containers for mixing
Soft, wide brush
Softening brush
Scrubbed potatoes in
   various sizes
Kitchen knife or
   scalpel
Ivory black artist's
   acrylic
Small roller and paint
   tray
Clean cloth
Medium artist's brush

Using the latex brush, apply a base coat of white latex, and leave to dry for 2–4 hours. For the background stripes, either choose 2 off-the-shelf latex colors, or mix your own: use white latex as a base, with a touch of raw sienna artist's acrylic for the pale color, and yellow ochre for the darker color. Using the wide brush, paint the darker stripes first, brushing out the edges while still wet. Do not attempt to make these too even: any irregularities will contribute to the overall effect. Before these stripes have dried completely, paint in the paler stripes, and blend the edges with the darker ones, using a dry softening brush. (If the area to be painted is large, complete the alternate stripes in stages.) Allow to dry for 2 hours.

1 Cut the potatoes in half, and, using the tip of the kitchen knife or scalpel, "draw" shapes onto the cut surfaces. Cut some of the prints in relief and others as "solid" areas, and remove the unwanted potato. Make several of each print, and use different sizes of potato.

3 Holding the potato firmly, use it to make several randomly placed prints on the wall: the paint will become fainter with each print, but this will contribute to the natural effect. Re-roll the potato with more paint as necessary. Repeat the process with the different potato cuts, varying the directions and layout of the prints. Wipe the potatoes with a cloth from time to time, and discard them when the prints begin to lose definition.

2 Squeeze a small quantity of ivory black artist's acrylic into the paint tray and roll the roller through it, ensuring that it is coated evenly. Select one of the cut potatoes and roll the black paint over the surface.

4 Fill in the "open" prints on the pale background stripes, using a medium artist's brush and the paint mixture used for the darker stripes.

THEATRICAL DRAWING ROOM

This delightfully informal trompe l'oeil scheme was inspired by the work of the French painter Christian Bérard and playfully recreates the world of theatrical set painting. Very simple techniques have been used to create a sense of space and light that is immediately appealing. The walls were first painted with a bright mustard yellow flat latex base coat and the fireplace, baseboards, and cornices with white latex. Once these were dry, a very free lining technique (see pages 96–7) was used to produce the faux paneling, utilizing several shades of burnt umber, dirty green, and white to give a "shadowed," three-dimensional effect.

The subtle floor tone provides a natural complement to the wall scheme. This was achieved with a tinted, varnish-based glaze applied and then grained with a simple "rocking" technique, before being softened out. A tinted, diluted undercoat provided the attractive "bleached" effect, and an oil-based varnish was applied to protect the finished surface.

Paneled walls

Using the latex brush, apply the mustard-yellow latex to the walls as a base color. When this is dry, paint in any existing features and moldings, such as the cornicing shown here, using 2 coats of white latex. Now mark out the trompe l'oeil panels.

Materials
Latex brush
Mustard-yellow and
   white flat latex paint
Pencil
Steel measuring tape
Level
Plumbline
Pair of compasses or
   length of string and
   a thumbtack
Pointed fitch
Cobalt blue, cadmium
   yellow, white and
   burnt umber artist's
   acrylics
Acrylic scumble glaze
Mahlstick (see page
   140 for description)
   or straight-edge

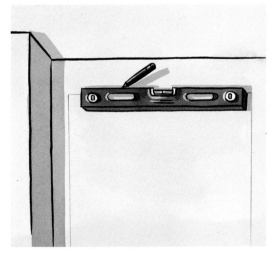

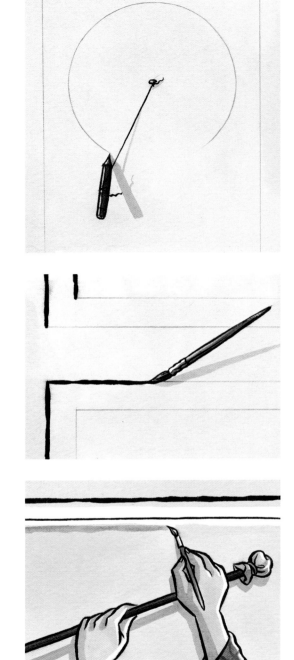

2 Find the center of each panel by laying a straight-edge across each diagonal, and marking the point at which the lines cross. Use a pair of compasses, or a pencil attached to a piece of string, to mark out the double circles, fastening the string at the center of each panel with a thumbtack if using the latter. The outer circle should just reach the sides of the panel. Measure carefully to keep the circles in each panel to the same dimensions.

3 Using a pointed fitch, paint in the panels, taking the pencil lines as your guide. To achieve the slightly three-dimensional effect shown here, use several different shades, from plain white flat latex paint, through a dirty green color mixed from cobalt blue, cadmium yellow and white artist's acrylics. Make the darkest shadow from neat burnt umber artist's acrylic mixed with just a few drops of water and acrylic scumble. As a general rule, position the darkest shading nearest the main light source and the lightest furthest away. Hold the brush lightly and allow the lines to flow naturally, without trying too hard to get them straight.

1 Work out a convenient panel size which can be repeated evenly around your walls. Using a steel measuring tape and pencil, indicate where the edges of the panels are to fall, then lightly join up the marks with the help of a level and plumbline to ensure that the lines are exactly horizontal or vertical.

4 If you are worried about working free-hand, use either a straight-edge or a mahlstick, a length of wood with a padded end, to steady your hand as you work. Use the straight-edge or mahlstick to rest your hand as you work rather than using it as a ruler. Once the paneling is complete, other features can be lined using the same techniques to complete the scheme.

Bleached faux pine floor

Prepare the floor surface for painting, as appropriate (see pages 194–8). Here, the floor consisted of plain wooden floorboards. Using the 3½in (9cm) brush, apply 2 even, solid coats of white eggshell, allowing each coat to dry for 24 hours. Prepare a glaze by tinting some white oil-based undercoat with a small amount of yellow ochre and raw sienna artist's oil pigments, being careful to mix the pigments thoroughly to avoid the possibility of streaking. Now add some satin oil-based varnish, at a ratio of 1:3 parts undercoat to varnish, and mix thoroughly once again.

Materials

3½in (9cm) brush	Containers for
White eggshell paint	mixing
White oil-based	Soft, wide brush
undercoat	Rubber "rocker"
Yellow ochre and raw	Softening brush
sienna artist's oil	Paint thinner
paints	Clean rags
Satin oil-based varnish	Varnish brush

1 Using the wide brush, apply the glaze evenly over one floorboard. Take the rubber "rocker" in your hand as shown: the open edge will be the "leading" edge through the glaze.

2 Draw the "rocker" through the wet glaze, adjusting its angle by rocking it back and forth as you work, to imitate the natural "grained" pattern of the wood. As soon as you have finished each board, lightly drag the dry softening brush through the pattern: this will remove any thick deposits of glaze left behind by the "rocker," and will provide greater subtlety in the overall effect. Move on to the next board, and repeat the process. Clean the "rocker" and softener at frequent intervals using a clean rag dipped in paint thinner, to remove paint as it builds up. When the whole floor is complete, leave it to dry for 16 hours.

3 Dilute more white undercoat up to 1:1 with paint thinner (the higher the ratio of the solvent to undercoat, the greater the translucency will be). Using a clean brush, apply a coat of this mixture to soften or "knock back" the grained effect. This will also help you achieve the required bleached-out appearance. Leave to dry overnight. Finish the floor by applying 4 coats of satin varnish to seal and protect the surface, allowing each coat to dry for 16 hours before applying the subsequent coat.

EMPIRE-STYLE SALON

The intricate paneling in this Louis XV-style salon could have been worked centuries ago. Not only is it contemporary, however, but it is not paneling at all— simply a clever use of trompe l'oeil, a three-dimensional effect created on a flush surface. To create this illusion, the way in which paint was used on the "paneling" was dictated by the natural fall of light and shadow in the room. The stylized floor decoration complements the wall decor perfectly, its "carpet" created by a mixture of painting and stenciling using tinted glazes.

Materials
Latex brush
White satin latex paint
Pale lemon yellow flat
 latex paint
Acrylic scumble glaze
Containers for mixing
Soft, wide brush or
 acrylic glazing brush
Softening brush
Steel measuring tape
Graph paper
Pencil
Ruler
Level
Plumbline
White and raw umber
 artist's acrylics
2 fine artist's brushes
Straight-edge
 (optional)
Low-tack masking
 tape (optional)
Satin oil-based
 varnish
Varnish brush

Trompe l'oeil paneling

Using the latex brush, apply 2 coats of white latex to the walls and ceiling, allowing each coat to dry for 2–4 hours. Prepare a glaze from 2 parts pale lemon latex, 7 parts acrylic scumble glaze and 1 part water (see page 83 for more about mixing glazes). Using a wide brush or acrylic glazing brush, apply the glaze over the whole surface, softening it out as you do, then leave to dry for 24 hours before applying a second coat.

On graph paper, draw a scaled version of the walls, marking in any features such as windows and a fireplace. Then draw in the cornicing, dado rail and baseboards, and finally the panels, working from the center of each wall for symmetry. Measure out the design of the cornicing, dado rail and baseboards on the walls in pencil, using the level and the plumbline.

Mark out the outlines of the individual panels and then the double moldings of each panel, within these outlines. These will be the areas in which highlights and shadows are painted in order to achieve the three-dimensional effect. Mark in mitered corners on each panel, as shown.

From the direction of the light (here shown coming from the upper right of the panel), establish which 2 edges of the "molding" will represent highlights, and which will depict shadows (see page 119). Using white for the highlights, and raw umber artist's acrylic for the shadows, and diluting each with a little water, paint these in using fine artist's brushes, either working free-hand or using a straight-edge for the straight sections, and mitering the corners. Alternatively, for sharper edges, fix low-tack masking tape on either side of each line before painting. Follow the same principle for the cornicing, dado rail and baseboards. Leave the finished painting to dry overnight. Finish and protect the work with a coat of satin oil-based varnish.

Materials

Latex brush
Pale lemon yellow, turquoise and red flat latex paint
Acrylic scumble glaze
Yellow ochre and raw umber artist's acrylics
Containers for mixing
String
Chalk
Thumbtacks
Graph paper
Pencil
Ruler
Triangle
Large pair of compasses (optional)
Small brush
Oiled stencil board or clear acetate
Stencil-cutting materials (see page 98)
Low-tack masking tape
Saucer
Stencil brush
Paper towels
Satin semi-gloss oil-based varnish
Varnish brush

Empire-inspired floor

Prepare the floor surface for painting, as necessary (see pages 194–8). Then, using the latex brush, apply 2 base coats of pale lemon yellow latex, allowing each coat to dry for 2–4 hours before applying the next. Mix a glaze from 2 parts of the same latex, 7 parts acrylic scumble, 1 part water and a little yellow ochre artist's acrylic. For the central panel and the interlocking circles, you will also need to make a turquoise glaze for the border on which the circles sit and one for the red border. This was "dirt-ied" by the addition of a little raw umber artist's acrylic.

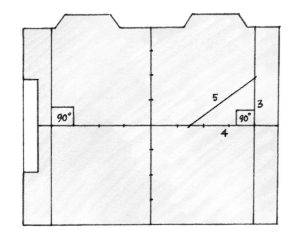

1 Square off the floor to create one square for each pattern repeat. To find the central point of the floor, find the mid-points at opposite walls and fix lengths of chalked string from one to the other with thumbtacks. Pull the strings tight and snap them on the floor to leave lines: the point at which they cross is the center. Working to scale on graph paper, plan the number of repeats in each direction, working from the center outwards. Mark off the squares along the lines, as shown. At the last points before the walls, mark lines at right-angles to the main axes. Use a triangle for the right-angle, or plot out by measuring 3 units along one line and 4 along the other: a line drawn between these points should measure 5 units. Mark off the squares as before.

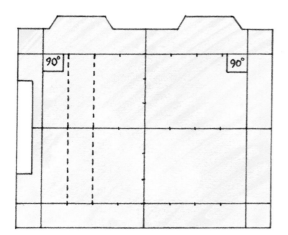

2 Draw in all the lines in one direction by joining up the points. Mark off squares along the outer lines as before, and complete the grid by joining the points. Transfer the paper grid to the floor itself, in pencil. For the circles in the outer border, draw a line along the middle of the border (the centers of the circles will sit here). Starting at one end of a long side, set a pair of compasses from the center line to draw a circle that just touches the border lines on either side. Draw the next circle overlapping the first, and so on, around the border. Position the corner circles so that they just touch the outer edges of the border. Using the small brush, apply the prepared tinted glazes to fill in the circles, border and central panel.

3 For the Empire leaf border, first use the pair of compasses (or pencil, string and thumbtack) to draw a circle in each corner of the border. For the leaf design, cut out a stencil from oiled stencil board or acetate: this should be a maximum of 12in (30cm) long for ease of use. Hold the stencil over the border and mark 2 registration marks at each end (see Greek wave border, page 149). Paint in the border using the brownish-red glaze and leave to dry for 24 hours. Fix the stencil in position at the end of one side with low-tack masking tape, pour some pale yellow latex into a saucer and stencil the leaf pattern (page 101). Leave each section to dry for 2 minutes before repositioning the stencil to overlap the previous one, and complete the stenciling in this way. Mask off the outer edges of the border corners with masking tape and, working freehand, carefully stencil the areas around the circles. Remove the masking tape, and leave to dry for 24 hours. Apply 4 coats of satin varnish, allowing each to dry for 24 hours before applying the next.

TOWNHOUSE SUITE

Broad stripes in fresh blue and creamy yellow contribute to the peaceful ambience of this well-proportioned drawing room. The stripes and white-painted floor were carried through the house and on into the bedroom, and consist of colored glazes applied over a tinted all-over glaze to provide a soft, translucent glow; they were "aged" by the application of randomly brushed patches of raw sienna. At dado height, a stenciled wave border provides a touch of contrast with its fluid lines, while the area beneath was painted with plain blue glaze. The beautifully understated floor was painted with a yellow-tinted undercoat, then coated with protective satin varnish.

Blue-and-white stripes

Materials
Latex brush
White satin latex paint
Creamy yellow flat
 latex paint
Acrylic scumble glaze
Containers for mixing
Soft, wide brush or
 acrylic glazing brush
Cobalt-blue flat
 latex paint
Artist's acrylics for
 tinting (optional)
Pencil
Level
Low-tack masking
 tape
Steel measuring tape
Plumbline
Softening brush
Raw sienna artist's
 acrylic

Using the latex brush, apply 2 coats of white latex over the entire wall surface, allowing each coat to dry for 2–4 hours. Mix a glaze of 2 parts creamy yellow latex, 7 parts acrylic scumble and 1 part water (see page 83 for more about mixing glazes). Separate this into 2 containers, and further dilute one quantity 3:1 with water. Use the wide brush or acrylic glazing brush to apply this diluted glaze loosely over the white base, and leave to dry overnight. Prepare a glaze for the blue stripes to the same proportions as above using cobalt-blue latex and adding acrylic scumble and water (the creamy stripes will be painted with the remaining yellow glaze). Adjust the shade of both glazes, if required, by adding touches of artist's acrylics in appropriate colors.

1 Decide on the height of the wave border—here it was positioned at about 38in (95cm) from the floor—and using a level, draw a horizontal line around the room. Run a strip of low-tack masking tape along the bottom of this line. Measure the length of each wall, and calculate the width of the stripes so that they will fit uniformly around the room. With the aid of a plumbline, lightly draw in these guidelines using a pencil.

2 Using a clean brush or acrylic glazing brush, paint in the blue stripes freehand with the prepared glaze, working with short, vertical strokes

and leaving soft, slightly uneven edges. While still wet, use the softening brush to pull off some of the glaze and soften out the finish. Leave to dry for 24 hours. Repeat the process for the pale stripes. When these are dry, mix a thin glaze of 3:1 acrylic scumble and water, tint this with a little raw sienna artist's acrylic, and brush it on in uneven patches to "age" the walls.

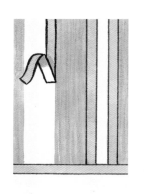

3 If you would prefer better-defined stripes for a rather more formal effect, apply masking tape along the vertical guidelines before you start painting. Paint the blue stripes first, leave to dry, then carefully remove the tape before placing more strips of tape in position ready to paint in the contrasting creamy stripes.

Greek wave border

Refix the masking tape at the base of the stripes, ensuring that it sits directly on top of, rather than just below, the line. Using a soft, wide brush or acrylic glazing brush and the glaze left over from the blue stripes, paint over the lower section of the wall up to the base of the stripes, then use the softening brush as before to pull off some of the glaze and lighten the overall effect. Leave to dry overnight.

Materials
Cobalt-blue flat latex
  paint
Acrylic scumble glaze
Containers for mixing
Soft, wide brush or
  acrylic glazing brush
Softening brush
Steel measuring tape
Pencil
Level
Paper
Low-tack masking
  tape
Oiled stencil board or
  clear acetate
Stencil-cutting tools
  (see page 98)
Ultramarine artist's
  acrylic
Saucer
Stencil brush
Paper towels
Medium artist's
  brush
White flat latex paint
Fine artist's brush

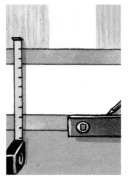

1 Measure down approximately 6in (15cm) from the base of the stripes. Using the level and a pencil, mark a line around the walls: this will represent the lower edge of the border. Mask off the bottom edge of the border. On paper, draw a 18in (45cm) long section of the wave repeat pattern (each wave should be the same). This section should be about 4½in (12cm) in height, leaving a ⅝in (1.5cm) gap at both top and bottom for the white border lines. Transfer this to oiled stencil board or acetate, and cut out the stencil (see page 98).

2 Hold the stencil against the border area and make registration marks at either end, aligning these with the inner edges of the masking tape. Cut V-shaped notches if using stencil board, or make short pencil lines on acetate. Fix the stencil in position at one end of a wall, using masking tape. Mix a glaze as for the dado area, adding ultramarine artist's acrylic and using only half the quantity of water for a darker shade. Place some glaze in a saucer, and stencil the border (see page 101). Allow each section to dry for about 2 minutes before repositioning the stencil to overlap the previous one. When complete, carefully remove the masking tape and leave to dry overnight. Fix new tape on either side of the border edges, and use the medium

artist's brush to paint in solid lines of white latex. Use full-strength blue latex and the fine artist's brush to paint a thin "shadow" beneath the white lines. Finally, add an extra coat of the denser, ultramarine-tinted glaze to both the dado and baseboard to give them additional weight.

Painted floor

The airy scheme of striped walls and white-painted floor was carried through the house to enhance both the drawing room and the bedroom, giving a wonderful sense of continuity and freshness.

To recreate the painted floor, first prepare the floor surface for painting, as necessary (see pages 194–8). Here, the surface was sanded right back to the bare wood. Dilute some white undercoat with paint thinner at a ratio of 1:1, then add sufficient yellow ochre artist's oil paint to soften the color slightly (only a very small amount of the pigment will be required, although the exact amount will depend on the final color effect you wish to obtain).

Materials
White oil-based undercoat
Paint thinner
Yellow ochre artist's oil paint
Container for mixing
Soft, wide brush
Clean rags
Satin oil-based varnish
Varnish brush

1 Using the brush, apply the undercoat mixture to the floor, working in long strokes along the direction of the wood grain, and brushing it in well.

2 Using a clean rag soaked in paint thinner, wipe back the boards as you work, to reveal some of the graining and knots in the wood. Use a new rag as necessary when it becomes paint-filled. Leave to dry overnight. Apply 4 coats of satin varnish to seal and protect the surface, allowing each to dry for 16 hours before applying the next.

SILHOUETTED SALON

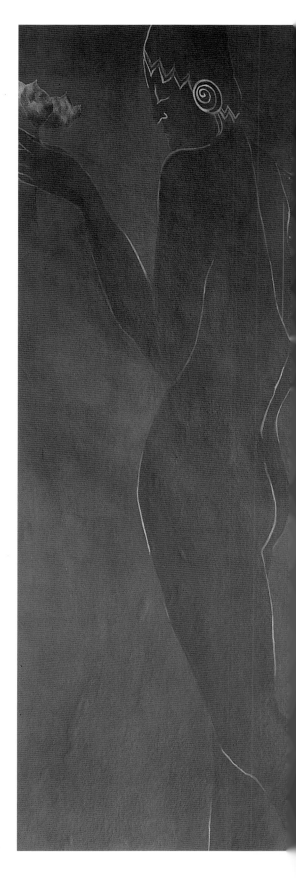

Barely defined figures moving silently across the walls, brushed in gleaming gold on indigo, give a ghost-like aura to this salon. A dark blue glaze was used for the wall area, with the color deepened for the borders, framing the silhouettes. Gold powder and acrylic scumble glaze were mixed for the linework and flowers, and a bold touch of Venetian red along the lower border and on the stems of the flowers adds bright highlights.

Materials

Latex brush
White satin latex paint
Dark blue flat latex
  paint
Acrylic scumble glaze
Turquoise, Venetian
  red and burnt sienna
  artist's acrylics
Containers for mixing
Soft, wide brush or
  acrylic glazing brush
Softening brush
Steel measuring tape
Pencil
Level
Low-tack masking
  tape
2 fine artist's brushes
Large sheet(s) or roll
  of tracing paper
Spray-mounting
  fixative
Carbon or transfer
  paper
Clean cloth
Gold powder or gold
  acrylic paint
Satin and matte
  acrylic varnish
Varnish brush

Salon walls

Using the latex brush, apply 2 coats of white latex over walls and ceiling, allowing each coat to dry for 2–4 hours. Mix a glaze from 2 parts dark blue latex, 7 parts acrylic scumble and 1 part water, adding touches of turquoise, Venetian red and burnt sienna artist's acrylics to create an indigo shade (see page 83 for more about mixing glazes). Using a wide brush or acrylic glazing brush, apply the glaze over walls and ceiling, softening the brushstrokes with a dry softening brush. Leave for 24 hours, then repeat. Decide on the silhouette positions, then, using a level, draw in the outer borders. Run low-tack masking tape along each line. Tint the remaining blue glaze with further touches of artist's acrylics to make a deeper indigo, and apply another coat to the border areas (leaving the first to dry for 24 hours). When dry, remove the tape. Apply 2 fresh strips of tape, with a narrow margin between them, near the top of the lower border, and use a fine artist's brush and Venetian red artist's acrylic diluted with a little water to fill in the line. Leave to dry, then remove the tape.

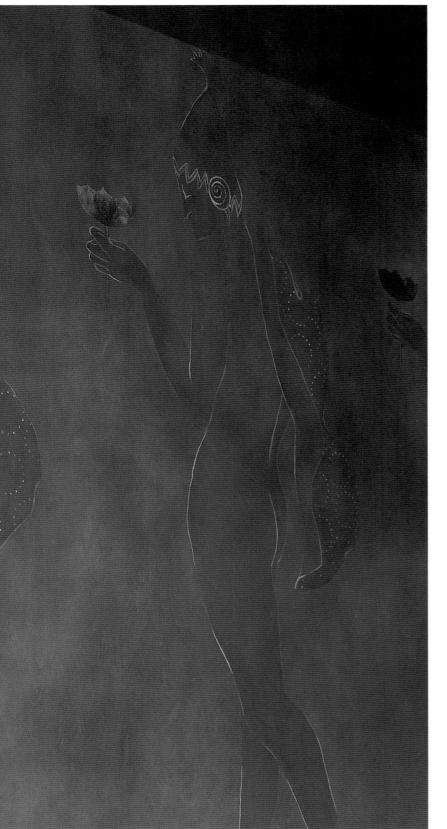

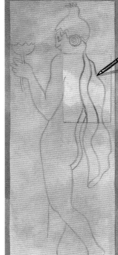

1 Select your source material for the silhouettes, and enlarge it on a photocopier to the required size (photocopy in sections and join them together, if necessary). Place tracing paper over the image and draw around the outline in pencil, adding any decorative details that you wish to include. Spray the back of the tracing with mounting fixative, position it on the wall (it is usually best to start in a corner) and lightly press it to the surface. Peel back the tracing at one edge, slip a sheet of carbon or transfer paper underneath, and then draw over the outline to transfer the silhouette to the wall. Continue like this, section by section, to transfer the whole image. Transfer all the silhouettes in this way, respraying the back of the tracing paper as necessary.

2 Take the glaze left over from painting the borders and, using a clean brush, fill in the silhouettes so that they stand out from the paler background, wiping back with a cloth in some areas to make the contrast more subtle: this will give the figures a more ghostlike quality. Leave to dry overnight. Mix the gold powder into acrylic scumble, and use this (or gold acrylic paint) and a fine artist's brush to pick out some of the outlines and motifs. Do this sparingly, or the elusive quality may be lost. Paint in the flower stems with Venetian red artist's acrylic, then leave to dry overnight. Apply a protective coat of varnish, using a satin finish on the borders and ceiling, and a matte finish on the central area.

GOLD BEDROOM

The classic geometry of diamonds, spaced evenly around the walls, adds a pleasing elegance to this bedroom. Reaching from the tops of the walls down to the border, the diamonds were painted with a gold mixed from gold powder and gloss varnish, over a green eggshell base. An off-white glaze was dragged between the diamonds to set off their gold sheen, and finally, the border was completed using the same green and gold color schemes.

Diamonds and border

Using the 3½in (9cm) brush, apply 2 coats of off-white eggshell over the entire wall, including the baseboards, allowing each coat to dry for at least 24 hours. Prepare the gold "paint" by mixing gold powder into gloss varnish. The more powder you add to the varnish, the more solid the gold finish will appear.

Materials

3½in (9cm) brush
Off-white eggshell
  paint
Gold powder
Gloss oil-based varnish
Containers for mixing
Steel measuring tape
Pencil
Level
Plumbline
String and chalk or a
  chalk line
Low-tack masking
  tape
2 medium brushes
Soft brush or clean
  cloth
Green and purple
  eggshell paint
Oil-based glaze
Paint thinner
Raw sienna artist's
  oil paint
Dragging brush
Oiled stencil board or
  clear acetate
Stencil-cutting
  materials (see
  page 98)
Saucer
Stencil brush
Paper towels

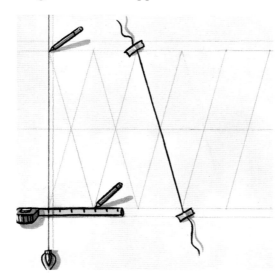

1 Start by working out the overall proportions of the scheme. Measure the walls and work out the widths of the diamonds, so that they will fit evenly around the room. Using a level and pencil, mark in the borders above and below the dia-monds, and the wider border beneath. Draw in another horizontal line equidistant between the 2 inner border lines, to mark the center of the diamond area. Based on your calculations, mark the top and bottom points of each diamond, using

cornices and archi-traves, can be painted in at the same time. Leave to dry for 24 hours, then paint over the thinner borders with the prepared gold mixture. Brush this on unevenly, and use a dry brush or cloth to pull off some of the mixture as you work to create an "antiqued" finish. Leave to dry overnight, then care-fully remove the tape. Paint the baseboards with purple eggshell.

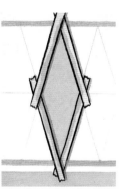

3 It may be tricky to mask off all the dia-monds at once, so mask off alternate shapes. Paint in the diamond shapes with green eggshell, leave to dry and then brush on the gold mixture, as for the borders. When dry, mask off the unpainted diamonds and repeat the process.

4 Mix a glaze of oil-based glaze and paint thinner, tinted with raw sienna artist's oil paint. Working on one shape at a time, use the 3½in (9cm) brush to apply the glaze, then a dragging brush to drag it (see pages 92–3) over the off-white areas. Leave for 24 hours. For a sharp-er line, you can apply masking tape along the inner edges of the diamonds before painting in these areas, trimming the tape into points at the top and bottom, to leave the off-white areas exposed, and removing the tape once the paint has dried. Repeat the whole process for the off-white area on the dado. For the gold balls along the lower border, draw and cut out a stencil from oiled stencil board or acetate (see page 98). Pour a little of the gold mixture into a saucer, and, using masking tape to fix the stencil to the border, stencil in the balls (see page 101), centering each one below a diamond.

a plumbline for accuracy. To form the diagonals, fix a length of chalked string from the top point of one diamond to the bottom of the next, and snap it against the wall to leave a line. Repeat this with all the diamonds.

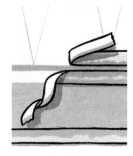

2 Run low-tack masking tape along the outer edges of the narrow border lines and the wider border at dado height. Then, using a medium brush and green eggshell, paint in the border areas. Any other obvious border areas in the room, such as

STONE-BLOCKED BATHROOM

The sensuous, tactile quality of smoothly polished, natural stone is brought into play as the key feature of this bathroom decor. This was achieved by exploiting the versatility of trompe l'oeil in a unique way to create a highly realistic result. Two glazes were applied over a light cream base to imitate the color of the stonework, and the blocks were drawn in and worked on individually to give each its own character and natural appearance. Shadows and highlights added around the "mortar" lines complete the illusion.

The painted walls

Materials
3½in (9cm) brush
Light cream eggshell
 paint
Oil-based glaze
Paint thinner
Raw umber and yellow
 ochre artist's oil
 paints
Containers for mixing
Soft, wide brush
Steel measuring tape
Pencil
Graph paper
Ruler
Level
Plumbline or T-square
Clean rags
Stippling or flat-
 bristled brush
White undercoat
Mid-green, burnt
 umber and white
 artist's oil paints
Fine artist's brush

Using the 3½in (9cm) brush, paint the walls with 2 coats of light cream eggshell, leaving each coat to dry for 24 hours before painting on any subsequent coats. Mix a glaze from oil-based glaze and paint thinner (see page 82 for more about mixing glazes). Separate this into 2 containers, and set one aside. Tint the remaining quantity of glaze with raw umber and a touch of yellow ochre artist's oil paints. Using the wide brush, loosely brush a coat of this glaze over the wall surfaces, softening out any obvious brushmarks as you work. Allow to dry for 24 hours.

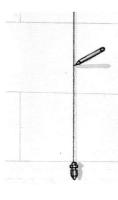

1 The proportions of the blocks will depend on the space available: measure the walls and work this out in a scaled-down version on graph paper. Using this as a guide, mark up the blocks on each wall in pencil. Use a level as a guide for the horizontals, and a plumbline or T-square for the vertical lines.

2 Working on each block in turn, apply more of the raw umber/yellow ochre glaze, but this time "manipulating" it to resemble stone and give each block an individual character. This is done by using the ragging technique (see pages 90–1) to pull off some of the glaze as it dries.

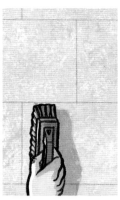

3 While the glaze is still wet, use the stippling or flat-bristled brush to stipple into the glaze at various points (see page 95), to enhance the natural-stone effect. When one block is complete, move on to the next and repeat the process. Try to create tonal differences between blocks, so that some are slightly darker than others. When you are satisfied with the overall effect, take the glaze set aside earlier, add a small quantity of white undercoat, and dilute the mixture 3:1 with paint thinner. Using the wide brush, apply this extra coat of glaze over the entire wall surface to leave a thin veil of color.

4 Mix the mid-green and burnt umber artist's oil paints to create a greenish-brown color for application as shadows, and use white artist's oil paints for the highlights, thinning each with a little paint thinner. Using the fine artist's brush, add the shadows and highlights just above and below the penciled "mortar" lines to give them greater impact. If these colors appear too stark, gently rub them back in a few places using a clean rag.

ANTIQUED FURNITURE

The versatility of paint as a medium is exploited to unusual effect on this basic wooden table. First, a thickly applied pink latex was swirled into patterns with a brush to achieve a heavily textured surface. When this was dry, a tinted, transparent oil-based glaze mixture was applied over the top, and worked carefully into the corners and crevices of the wood, to deepen the tone and create a surface resembling ancient, well-worn leather. To underline the newly opulent appearance of the table, the elegant barley-twist legs were finished with a coat of rich gold acrylic paint.

Painted table

Prepare the surface of the table for painting, as necessary (see pages 194–8). Using fine-grade sandpaper, give the whole surface a final thorough sanding to smooth it down, then wipe away every particle of dust using a clean cloth. Using a latex brush, apply a coat of white acrylic undercoat and leave to dry for 4 hours.

Materials
Fine-grade sandpaper
Clean cloth
Latex brush
White acrylic
  undercoat
Small, soft brush
Pink flat latex paint
Oil-based glaze
Raw umber artist's
  oil paint
Paint dryers
Container for mixing
Clean rags
Gold acrylic paint and
  small artist's brush
  (optional)
Semi-gloss oil-based
  varnish
Varnish brush

1 Using a soft brush, apply a thick layer of pink latex to the surface of the table. Then, holding the brush vertically, dab at the paint to create random swirling patterns with the bristles: your aim should be to create a heavily textured "relief." When you are satisfied with the effect, leave the paint for at least 24 hours until it is completely dry. If you wish, you can repeat the process with a second coat to create additional texture.

2 Tint some oil-based glaze to the desired shade using raw umber artist's oil paint. Paint dryers can be added if you wish to speed up the drying process. Using a clean rag, smear the glaze over the table, then use a small brush to push the glaze into awkward corners and cracks. Take another clean rag and lightly rub back the surface to remove excess glaze and complete the "aged" effect, then leave to dry undisturbed for 24 hours. If appropriate, apply a coat of gold acrylic paint to the table legs, using a small artist's brush. Finally, protect the table with 2 coats of semi-gloss oil-based varnish.

PAINTS ARE DESIGNED TO PERFORM DIFFERENT TASKS
ON DIFFERENT SURFACES. THIS CHAPTER WILL HELP
YOU CHOOSE THE RIGHT PAINTS, PRIMERS, AND
SOLVENTS FOR YOUR NEEDS.

directory
of paints and surfaces

WHATEVER WE DECIDE TO PAINT, inside or outside the house, three factors influence our choice of paint—the color, the finish, and the composition. Color decisions may be affected by the type of paint you have to use; 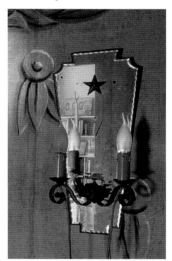 *for example, paints that are specifically designed for use on rough exterior walls come in a limited range of shades, while there is a huge variety of colors available for use on smooth plaster or interior woodwork.*

"Finish" is the term used to describe the surface texture of paint, from a high-gloss sheen to a vellum-like flat, and is a factor in determining a paint's durability as well as its appearance. The term "composition" refers to a paint's make-up—whether it is acrylic-, oil- or water-based—and conditions how long a paint takes to dry and what effects we can achieve with it, as well as where it can be applied. To make things simpler, the following chapter gives a breakdown of paint types, solvents, and primers, and advises which surfaces they can be used on to best effect.

When choosing a paint finish, consider the surrounding surfaces and objects. Here the soft furnishings and metallic-gold painted walls are complemented by the eggshell sheen of the lilac table.

OPAQUE FINISHES

Most standard decorating paint is opaque when used undiluted straight from the can. Oil-based versions generally have the texture of light cream, while many of the water-based latex paints are somewhat thicker, more the consistency of ketchup. However, both of these types of paint can usually be thinned by using one of a variety of different solvents (see page 167).

Thicker, non-drip varieties, such as one-coat latex paints, are also available. These are generally intended for use with rollers or brushes and should not be diluted. Although easy to use, they are not very versatile paints, and you will find them quite useless for carrying out broken-color and glazing techniques, and for achieving more sophisticated finishes.

FLAT FINISHES
These paints have a finish with absolutely no shine or sheen, rather like smooth, high-quality writing paper or chamois

leather. The greatest advantages of flat finishes are that they will help even out an irregular surface and will not shine when illuminated from an angle. However, they are not without their drawbacks, namely a tendency to collect dust and the fact that they are harder to wipe clean than eggshell, semi-gloss, or gloss paints.

Flat latex
Flat latex is the most commonly used variety, but the term is

used for a wide range of water-based decorating paints of varying textures and qualities. Unsuitable for use on metal, latex paints are primarily used on plaster. They are relatively inexpensive, quick to dry, and easily tinted, so are excellent for use in washes. Special anti-fungicidal versions are available for poorly ventilated kitchens and bathrooms. The surface of new, dry plaster can be sealed by painting on a

"mist" coat of latex thinned 1:1 with water, followed by a coat at full strength. Once these are dry, any other type of water-based paint can be used as a finish.

New-plaster latex
Specially formulated for use on new interior walls and ceilings, this latex allows the moisture in new plaster to escape rather than sealing the surface. Two coats are normally required.

One-coat latex

One-coat latex has a much higher opacity than standard latex paints and only one coat, rather than the more usual two, is required. However, it is less versatile than other latex paints, being unsuitable for use in many special paint techniques. You should try to avoid spreading out the paint too thinly, especially when overpainting a very bright color or a contrasting shade.

Flat oil paint

This has excellent coverage and consistency, and provides perhaps the most aesthetically pleasing finish on interior surfaces. For the best results, always use an undercoat followed by two top coats thinned with paint thinner. Flat oil paint should never be diluted thinner than the consistency of light cream. When painting with flat oil paint, ensure that all finishing brushstrokes are made towards the dominant source of light. Flat oil paint may only be available from specialist suppliers.

Undercoat

This is a flat, opaque paint which provides a non-porous ground for all oil-based finishing coats. Undercoat is only available in a very limited color range, but it is easily tinted.

Distemper

Often known as whitewash, this is one of the oldest forms of wall paint and gives a subtle finish on plaster over a wide range of textures. It is easy to remove but not very hardwearing. Distemper is rarely available from commercial suppliers, but soft distempers (claircolle and casein-based distemper) are easy to make at home (see page 201 for recipes) and can be tinted with artist's powder pigments or gouache paints.

Limewash

Similar to claircolle distemper, this is made using slaked lime instead of whiting and can be used to decorate exterior walls. Like distemper, it is not particularly hardwearing or waterproof and tends to rub off easily.

Traditionally used on rough cottage walls, distemper and lime-wash, either tinted or natural white, look very effective on undulating plaster.
(FAR LEFT)

Distemper offers a cool, subtle finish that works well with understated colors and natural textures.
(BELOW)

GLOSS FINISHES

These types of paint have a high reflective shine. They are almost always oil-based, with the exception of some of the newer acrylic decorating paints, and are therefore fairly slow-drying paints.

EGGSHELL FINISHES

These are often referred to as "satin finishes" and have a soft, diffused sheen. They are silky to the touch, and so offer an excellent base coat over which other paint effects can be applied.

Oil-based gloss

The terms "high gloss," "gloss," "semi-gloss," and "hard gloss" are used to describe different levels of shine. In general, the shinier the gloss, the more durable the finish. Gloss paint can be used on both interior and exterior surfaces including woodwork and metal. It is highly resistant to water and dirt, making it ideal for use on kitchen and bathroom walls, and it is easily washable. Gloss paint can be diluted with paint thinner, but should never be thinned down to a very runny consistency. Another advantage of gloss paint is that it is available in a wide color range.

Water-based eggshell

A non-porous, fast-drying paint, water-based eggshell is suitable for use both on interior walls and woodwork, and will last longer than flat latex on the latter. Water-based eggshell paint should never be diluted thinner than the consistency of light cream.

Oil-based eggshell

Oil-based eggshell paint gives a soft, sophisticated sheen to woodwork and walls and is suitable for many broken-color techniques (see pages 78–101). It is best applied in several thinned coats rather than a single thick layer, and requires an under-coat when used on wood. Like most gloss paints, it is fairly slow-drying.

Trade eggshell

Available only through specialist trade suppliers, this oil-based paint is superior to other types of eggshell, and is suitable for use on both wood-work and walls. When applying trade eggshell, take care to make all finishing brushstrokes toward the dominant source of light, as for flat oil paint.

High-gloss finishes, especially in bold colors, can look stunning. They are a particularly good choice for floors, being durable and waterproof.
(ABOVE)

UNUSUAL FINISHES

There is a specialist paint for virtually every type or condition of surface for which standard interior or exterior paints would be inappropriate or ineffective.

Textured paint

Textured paint is most commonly used to obliterate minor cracks in otherwise sound masonry or plaster. Available in a range of different textures, the roughest varieties can cover cracks up to ⅛in (2mm) wide and should be applied with a coarse roller. Those with finer textures should be applied with a synthetic fiber roller or a standard brush.

The main drawback to this paint is that it is extremely difficult to remove.

Water-based masonry paint

This is suitable for all types of sound, clean masonry including bricks (provided they have already been painted), stone, concrete, cement rendering, and stucco. It can also be used to paint over latex and cement paint. Two coats are usually required and they can be applied using a brush, roller, or spray.

Oil-based masonry paint

Like its water-based counterpart, this can be used over all masonry surfaces. Although it takes longer to dry, it has greater coverage over most surfaces and can be recoated sooner than water-based masonry paint. Two coats are usually required and they can be applied using a brush, roller, or spray.

Reinforced masonry paint

This is either oil- or water-based and can be used on all the masonry surfaces described above. It has a denser texture and gives less coverage than standard masonry paints, but you may only need to apply one coat. If you require two coats, wait at least 24 hours before applying the second.

Cement paint

Supplied in the form of a powder which is then mixed with water, this provides an efficient and hardwearing paint for interior use in cellars, garages and workshops. On exteriors it can be applied over all types of sound, clean masonry including stone, concrete, cement rendering and stucco. However, unlike masonry paints, it is not suitable for use over latex or oil-based paints. It dries to a flat finish and is touch dry in one to two hours, and can be recoated after 24 hours. Two coats are the normal requirement and these can be applied with either a brush or roller.

A vivid blue flat paint used on a cement wall is intensified by bright sunlight. (BELOW)

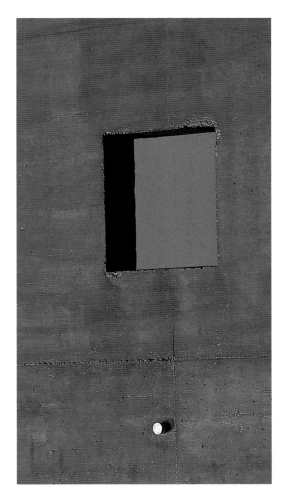

Metallic paint

This paint is designed specifically for use on metal and contains either powdered copper, gold or bronze. Generally applied at full strength, it is water resistant and can withstand temperatures of up to 212°F (100°C) (boiling point).

Hammered-finish paint

Hammered-finish paint is designed specifically for use on metal. It leaves a textured surface and consists of aluminum particles, heat-hardened glass, and resins. It should be applied in two unthinned coats and does not require use of a primer or

undercoat, even if you are applying it over previously rusted surfaces. A version with similar properties but providing a smoother finish is also available.

Fluorescent paint

Fluorescent paint is generally used in the industrial sector, and is also applied to vehicles and aircraft for safety and recognition purposes. It is also available in artist's acrylics for some decorative effects, and

artist's gouache, in which form it is often used for display work. However, the latter is not colorfast.

Non-slip paint

Non-slip paint is designed to provide a firm foothold on surfaces such as metal stairways and fire escapes. Always use a primer and be sure to read the manufacturer's instructions carefully before application.

Asphaltum

The prime function of this bitumen-based paint is to protect exterior storage tanks and metal piping. It is usually black, but a limited range of other colors is available, along with a modified variety containing aluminum. Brushes used for asphaltum should never be used for other paints. Ashphaltum may not be readily available; ask your paint supplier about substitutes.

An area of silver metallic paint, applied over a pewter-gray wall, acts as a waterproof splashback. The underlying rough wall texture gives the metallic paint the look of beaten tin.
(ABOVE)

PRIMERS AND SOLVENTS

A primer is a sealing agent applied to a surface to prevent any subsequent paint coat being absorbed or rejected by it. Primers are necessary on the great majority of previously unpainted surfaces.

Solvents are basically thinning agents which can be mixed with paints and varnishes to alter their consistency so that they flow more easily and cover larger areas, but they are also used as cleaning agents. Water is the solvent for all water-based paints. All chemical solvents are toxic and flammable, so you should take suitable precautions when using them and avoid inhaling them or getting them on your skin. Empty containers or solvent- and paint-soaked rags have been known to combust spontaneously if thrown away into plastic bags which are then left out in the sun. They should be disposed of responsibly and in accordance with local regulations.

PRIMERS

General-purpose primer

If you intend to use oil-based paint, this can be used on old plaster and plasterboard. It is also suitable for metal, brick, stone, cement rendering, concrete, wood, chipboard, hardboard and plywood, and can be used on radiators, provided they have previously been painted with paint other than radiator enamel. Thin if necessary using paint thinner.

Alkali-resistant primer

This prevents alkaline salts from attacking oil-based paint. It is especially suitable for new plaster that has been dried and cured if you intend to finish it in oil-based paint, but can also be used on brick, stone, cement rendering, concrete, plaster and plasterboard.

Acrylic wood primer

A water-soluble primer for use on soft- and hardwoods, chipboard, hardboard and plywood. Two coats are necessary, and you should pay particular attention to the end grain. Some types may also be used as an undercoat.

Standard wood primer

This performs the same function as acrylic primer and can be thinned with paint thinner. It prevents oil-based paint soaking into the wood and provides a foundation for later coats.

Aluminum wood primer

Specifically designed for use on oily hardwoods, this is suitable for all types of exterior woodwork and can also be used to cover creosote. This type of primer will only be found in specialist stores.

Zinc phosphate primer

Generally used on interior metalwork, this is suitable for priming ferrous metal, galvanized metal and aluminum, including the heads of nails.

Rust-inhibiting primer

This is for exterior use on bare ferrous metal and should be applied immediately after removing paint or rust, or to prevent rust forming on new metal. It is not suitable for use on galvanized metal or aluminum.

Quick-drying metal primer

Quick-drying metal primer can be used on all interior and exterior ferrous metals, but is not suitable for use on galvanized metal or aluminum.

Red oxide primer

A primer used mainly to prevent iron and steel from corroding, red oxide can be used before applying both water- and oil-based paints. It is a popular base color for gilding and bronzing.

Water-based metal primer

A quick-drying primer specially formulated for use on non-ferrous metals.

SOLVENTS

Paint thinner

Also known as mineral spirits, this is suitable for thinning all oil-based paints and varnishes without yellowing or distorting the color, and speeds their drying times. It is also the prime cleaning agent for brushes and equipment. If applied quickly, it can be used to remove paint from clothes without staining; the benzene-like smell can be eliminated by washing the garment in warm, soapy water.

Turpentine

Made from distilled pine-tree resin, turpentine is used largely by artists as a thinner for oil-based paint. It is much more expensive than paint thinner and is rarely indispensable in decorative wall painting; its drying time is slightly slower than paint thinner, but it is less likely to dull oil paint. It has a distinctive, pleasant odor.

Refined linseed oil

All oil paints were originally based on linseed oil. Today, with the exception of artist's oil paints, most oil-based decorating paint is suspended in other solutions, but linseed oil is still widely used in glaze techniques. It increases the fluidity and transparency of oil-based pigment by dispersing the grains, as well as slowing drying times and adding a glossy finish. Linseed oil is pale gold in color and has a sweet fragrance.

Universal brush cleaner

This is a solution used exclusively for cleaning both oil- and water-based paint from brushes and equipment. After cleaning, brushes should be washed in warm, soapy water, twirled to remove excess water and hung up to dry. This chemical should never be confused with chemical paint strippers.

TRANSLUCENT FINISHES

Decorating paint is not generally translucent except when it has been thinned extensively with varnishes or glazes. These give the thinned paint sufficient "body" to be durable. All varnishes and glazing media are naturally translucent, but although they are primarily used to protect surfaces, varnishes can also be tinted with varying amounts of paint. Scumble glazes are thicker versions of varnishes, dry more quickly, and are specifically designed to have paint added to them in varying amounts.

VARNISHES
Oil-based varnish
This is available in satin and gloss finishes and usually has a slightly yellowish tone, which softens and adds depth to the surface beneath. It is generally used over oil-based paints to give a hardwearing protective finish, and can be tinted with artist's oil paints and pigments. Always stir oil-based varnish carefully for 1–2 minutes before use, and take care not to apply it too fast as this will create air bubbles. Never shake a can of varnish instead of stirring it, as the action will create hundreds of air pockets, leading to cracking after application. On walls,

use two coats of satin or gloss varnish thinned to 3:1 parts

varnish to paint thinner. On floors, three coats is the absolute minimum, but it is advisable to use six. Although it takes longer to dry, gloss varnish gives by far the most durable finish, but if you want to tone down the shine,

apply a finishing coat of eggshell varnish over five gloss layers.

Polyurethane varnish
Polyurethane varnish is available in matte, satin, or gloss finishes and provides the hardest and most durable protective finish, although lacking the depth and mellow finish of other types of varnish. It can be thinned with paint thinner and is available in almost colorless form, which can be tinted with artist's oil paints and pigments, or in colored finishes. Polyurethane is normally touch dry in two to three hours, and recoatable in five or six, so this type of

varnish is particularly useful on floors and work surfaces. Avoid leaving too much time between coats, as the varnish will not adhere well to a completely dry surface. Polyurethane is less elastic than other varnishes, so it needs to be rubbed down with particular care.

Acrylic varnish
Acrylic varnish is available in matte, satin, or gloss finishes. Although it appears a slightly cloudy white in the tin, it provides a clear finish so long as it is not applied too thickly. Acrylic varnish does not dry much quicker than oil-based varnishes, but because it is water-soluble it

becomes touch dry much faster, especially if you have thinned it down. Acrylic varnish can be applied over both oil- and water-based paints so long as they are completely dry.

Crackle varnish
This imitates the effect of very old varnish or paint which has cracked over time. It actually involves the application of two varnishes: first a coat of slow-drying, transparent, tinted antiquing varnish is applied to the surface, followed by a quick-drying cracking varnish. This latter layer cracks as it dries and produces fine lines that can be tinted with polish or oil paint.

GLAZES
Oil-based glaze
Oil-based glaze is like a very loose and malleable varnish and provides a translucent finish. It is thinned with paint thinner and can be tinted, and is brushed on or wiped off in one or several layers in decorating techniques such as color-washing, marbling, and woodgraining. Allow each layer of glaze to dry before painting on the next coat.

Acrylic scumble glaze
This is similar to oil-based glaze, although looser in consistency and generally cloudy white in its concentrated form. It is used in the same way as oil-based glaze, but is thinned with water and tinted with water-based pigments and paints.

Crackle glaze
This is a colorless, generally opaque, glaze that is applied between two contrasting layers of emulsion paint. When the top paint coat dries, the glaze causes it to crack, revealing the base color beneath. Transparent crackle glaze can be used in a similar way to oil-based crackle varnish (left).

Crackle varnish produces a delicate web of fine lines that can be enhanced with artist's oil colors.
(FAR LEFT)

Sections of this wall have been coated with layers of gesso, then tinted with layers of varnished glazes. A gold stenciled frieze adds the finishing touch.
(BELOW)

TINTING MEDIA

Tinting meáns altering the color of a paint or varnish by adding a little of another color. This can be done to some extent with ordinary decorating paint, but artist's materials are specifically designed for this purpose and are much more effective, because a relatively small amount goes a very long way. There is also a vastly superior color range. Unlike decorating paints, they are rarely sold in bulk, but are available in tubes or small tubs from art supply stores.

Artist's powder pigments

These are finely ground pigments, many of which are derived from refined clays and minerals, which can be used for tinting all kinds of paints and glazes. They are available in the widest and most sophisticated of all color ranges and because their names are internationally recognized, the

colors remain consistent whatever the brand or type of paint. They should be used cautiously as the colors are very strong, and the pigment must be well dispersed before use. The coarser pigments can be ground down further using a pestle and mortar to make this process easier.

Artist's oil pigments

These are usually sold in tubes and tubs from artist's suppliers and are generally used for oil painting. They are highly concentrated, consisting of refined pigment bound in linseed oil, and are ideal for tinting any oil-based paint used in decorative painting, but the pigment must be well

dispersed to avoid streaking. This is best done by first mixing the pigment into a little paint thinner (or linseed oil if you wish to slow down the drying process) with a palette knife, before adding it gradually to the decorating paint.

Powder paints

These should not be confused with artist's powder pigments. Powder paints are

much cheaper because they have a great deal of filler mixed in with the pigment, but the colors are somewhat crude, rather gritty in texture, and their coverage is patchy and often weak. Powder paints are generally used in schools because of their low cost, but are not suitable for any serious painting work.

Poster paints

These water-soluble paints have a strong but rather limited color range, and were traditionally used for producing bright areas of color on paper or cardboard. They are less expensive and less subtle than gouache, but are effective for tinting water-based paint.

Signwriter's paints

These are fast-drying, free-flowing oil-based paints traditionally used for the lettering on advertising boards, and are ideal for any precise, detailed work such as lining and woodgraining (see pages 96–7 and 112–15). They have a semi-gloss finish and are available

in a wide range of colors. If applied over a base color, only one coat is necessary.

Artist's acrylics

Developed in the 1950s, these are excellent, water-soluble, plastic-based artist's pigments. Highly concentrated, they are generally

translucent and are available in an almost identical color range to their oil-based counterparts. They are also cheaper, although they give slightly less coverage. Acrylics dry rapidly, making them suitable for sharp-edged work such as stenciling, but retarders are available if you need to slow down the drying process.

Gouache paints

Water-based pigments used widely by artists, illustrators and designers, these are available in a range of colors almost as wide as that of artist's oils. They make excellent tinting

agents for water-based decorating paints, and are probably the most versatile of all water-soluble pigments for washes.

Metallic powders

These are generally available through artist's suppliers and specialist decorating

shops. Supplied as gold, silver, bronze or gray powder pigments, they can be mixed with glaze media or with paint

to give a concentrated metallic effect or to add a metallic tint to another color.

Universal tints

These can be used to tint both oil- and water-based paints. They are easy to mix, and very powerful and concentrated, so only a tiny amount is required to tint a relatively large quantity of paint.

A sea-green color-washed wall perfectly sets off a distressed crackle-glazed wooden frame.
(FAR LEFT)

Evoking an ancient Cretan fresco, a simple freehand wave design crowning a panel of bright yellow, turns plain stonework and cement into a decorative feature.
(BELOW)

EXTERIORS

Protection is the prime purpose of painting the exterior of your house, whether you are painting walls and guttering or window frames and doors. Wind, water and sunlight all wreak damage on exposed wood and ferrous metal, so it is especially important to carry out any painting work properly and to keep it in good repair. The exterior paintwork of a house can look as attractive as anything you paint inside, so choose its color with care, taking into account the age of your house, its character and any regional traditions.

The ideal weather for painting outside is warm and overcast. Try to avoid painting in bright sunlight as the sun will pucker the paint and dry it too quickly, and on wet days both oil- and water-based paints will be diffi-

cult to apply. If you have to work on a sunny day, follow the sun around the house, so that its warmth has had a chance to dry out the night's damp before you start painting.

PAINTS

Masonry paints

Masonry paints can be either oil- or water-based—the former are sometimes referred to as solvent-based paints—and most have a flat finish or a soft sheen. They have a latex-like, creamy consistency and often give a stucco effect. They can be used over both latex and oil-based paints, but may not bond well to surfaces painted with the latter; make sure that the previous layers of paint are sound and dry. If you have to paint brickwork, always use masonry paint, as it is specially formulated to be less harmful to the structure of the bricks than other types of paint.

Exterior latex paints

Water-based exterior latex paints are thinner and easier to apply than masonry paints. There are many types available, from those with flat finishes to textured varieties containing mica or quartz to give a sand-like finish.

Oil-based paints

These are used on all exterior woodwork. Gloss varieties should be applied over a primer and undercoat. Eggshell paints should not be used on exteriors unless specifically marketed as exterior-graded semi-gloss paints. For the most durable finish on exterior woodwork, apply two or three thinned coats over a primer and undercoat before painting on a final coat at full strength. Be careful not to overthin the paint and avoid painting in direct sunlight, as this can cause the paint to pucker or blister.

Specialist oil-based paints include floor paint, for use on tiles, concrete and stone flooring; non-slip paint, which provides a secure footing on slippery metal; and metal paints, some of which (for example hammered-finish paint) have their own special solvents.

PAINTS	SURFACES									
Primers	Wood	Metal	Brick	Stone	Cement rendering	Concrete	Stucco	Latex & oil paint	Cement paint	Pipes & guttering
General purpose	•	•	•	•	•	•	•			
Alkali-resistant			•	•	•	•	•			
Acrylic and standard wood primer	•									
Aluminum wood primer	•									
Rust-inhibiting primer		•								
Quick-drying metal primer		•								
Paints										
Water-based exterior latex paints			•	•	•	•	•	•		
Limewash			•							
Oil-based gloss	•									•
Textured paint			•	•	•	•	•			
Water-based masonry paint			•	•	•	•	•	•	•	
Oil-based masonry paint			•	•	•	•	•	•	•	
Reinforced masonry paint	•		•	•	•	•	•	•	•	
Cement paint				•	•	•	•			
Metallic paint		•								
Hammered-finish paint		•								
Non-slip paint	•	•	•	•		•				•
Asphaltum		•								

SURFACES
Masonry

Before you start painting, all masonry, whether stone, brick, cement rendering or stucco, should be prepared thoroughly. First, scrub it down

with a stiff brush to remove any loose material. Next, scrape off any moss or mold and treat with fungicide, then wash the whole area thoroughly with water. Fill any cracks and holes, and then seal the whole surface with stabilizing primer.

For undamaged surfaces, a general-purpose primer will be sufficient. Previously painted masonry should be repainted with the same type of paint. If you are painting over oil-based paint, clean it first with liquid sander or a household detergent. Always work from the top down, so that any cleaning or sealing agents flow down the wall, making your task gradually easier.

Brick

Brickwork, especially on old properties, should never be painted as this can cause damage to the structure of the wall. However, where brick has already been painted it is better to add another coat rather than attempt to remove the old paint.

Exterior metalwork

Exterior metalwork is usually ferrous in the case of railings, older piping and garden furniture, or aluminum in the case of window frames. Never paint over rust: use a wire brush and scraper to remove both rust and any loose, flaking

paint right back to shiny metal before painting. Ferrous metal should be coated with rust inhibitor or quick-drying metal primer. Give aluminum window frames a coat of zinc phosphate primer.

If the existing paint is perfectly sound, wash it down with a detergent solution, before rinsing and drying the metal. Rub down gloss paint with fine wet-and-dry paper to provide a key for the new paint, then apply undercoat and finish with oil-based paint.

Metalwork generally looks best painted in dark colors such as dark greens, blues, deep reds, and black. Paler colors tend to tarnish and will soon look shabby.

Pipes and guttering

To prepare cast-iron guttering for painting, brush out any leaves or debris then wash it clean. Coat the inside with asphaltum or an asphaltum substitute. If you wish to paint over old asphaltum, first use an aluminum primer so that the old asphaltum will not bleed through the new paint. Plastic pipes and guttering need to be washed and dried before painting with oil-based or exterior acrylic paints.

Metal garden furniture

If you want to paint very detailed metalwork, first remove the old paint with a chemical stripper (see pages 197–8). Alternatively, if the object is portable, either get it sandblasted commercially or use an industrial stripper. Once it is cleaned, either paint

it with a rust-inhibiting primer or use a rust converter, which will combine with the rust, leaving it inert in the form of iron phosphate.

Exterior woodwork

New woodwork should be sanded, treated with preservative, and primed with a compatible primer. After priming, fill any faults with an exterior-grade filler, followed by a primer. You can use general-purpose, standard, or acrylic wood primer, but aluminum wood primer is most suitable if you are painting on oily hardwood. If the wood has already been painted, wash it down with household detergent, rinse, then sand it lightly or paint with liquid sander to provide a key for the new paint. Ideally, apply primer, undercoat, and two coats of oil-based gloss. Undercoat is essential if you need to prevent an older paint color from showing through.

Windows

Small windows can be made to appear larger if you use white paint on the window frames and inner edges. Painting the bars of a window in the same color as the frame will make a short window appear longer, whereas painting the bars in a contrasting color will widen the window. Small-paned sash

windows, and patterned windows such as fanlights over doors, show up best when the wood is painted white or in a light color. Single-paned sash windows often look most

effective painted in deeper colors such as dark green, brown or black. Exterior louvered shutters can be painted a different color from the glazing bars of the windows, but this should match the color of the front door.

Doors

Front doors can either be painted as you choose to match windows, guttering and railings, or in a single contrasting color. Side doors, garage doors and hatch covers look best painted in the same color as the walls. Glazed doors, such as French

windows, should match the window frames. Unless you are using white, paint the door in a different color than its frame to prevent it from turning into a void where no modeling or detail is picked out. The colors should relate

to the surrounding walls, with cool colors used alongside warmer ones: for example, a chrome-green door with a white frame will look handsome with dark, sandy stone walls.

Weatherboarding

Always work from the top downward, whether the direction of the boards is horizontal or vertical, painting the under edge (or side edge of a vertical board) before the face, and being careful to coat any exposed end grain well, as it is more absorbent and so requires extra

protection. Try to work across as large an area as will allow you to keep the wet edge of the paint fresh, to avoid join marks showing in the paint. If the boards are relatively short (about 10ft/3m) you can paint them one at a time.

Ochre stucco accented by cream-painted cornerstones and cornices, and pale lime green shutters.
(ABOVE)

The traditional practice of painting doors and shutters to match creates an elegant symmetry. The black line at the base of the wall has a functional role, disguising the inevitable dirt and rain splashes.
(FAR LEFT, BELOW)

INTERIORS

Painting an interior is usually referred to as decoration, because although the paint functions as a protective coating, as on exterior walls, there is much greater scope for experimenting with pattern and color. As often as not, we choose the interior paintwork as much for aesthetic as practical reasons, hence the vast range of paints available, from thick one-coat paints to versatile artist's pigments.

Always start by making any necessary repairs. Paint can do many things, but gluing together a fractured structure is not one of them. Clear out as much of the furniture as you can and put drop cloths over the rest. If possible, remove rugs and carpets and lightly spray water over the floors to dampen down the dust, making it easy to sweep up. Protect tiled or wooden floors or carpets that cannot be removed with drop cloths.

With most types of paint it is best to work in well-ventilated surroundings, but beware of strong drafts which will create

dust. Never smoke while working or anywhere near drying paint, particularly if it is oil-based, as many paints and solvents are highly flammable. If you suffer from asthma or any breathing disorder, wear a respirator—a mask may not be sufficient to filter out irritating fumes. Try to avoid wearing wool, because its loose hairs have an exasperating habit of sticking to paintwork.

PAINTS
Interior latex
Most commonly used for painting plaster, all types of latex share the advantage of being easy to use and quick to dry. However, they are unsuitable for many broken-color techniques.

Oil-based paint
The prime difference between water- and oil-based paints is that the latter dry more slowly, cover a greater area and remain workable for appreciably longer than water-based varieties. The versatility of flat oil paint, undercoat, and eggshell and semi-gloss paints enables you to achieve most of the broken-color techniques and faux finishes associated with interior design, as well as a single, durable paint finish.

Oil-based gloss
This is primarily intended for use on woodwork and metal-work. Oil-based gloss is highly durable, although inclined to chip. It should be applied carefully with a brush over a primed and undercoated sur-face. Apply the paint sparingly, using criss-cross strokes and taking all the finishing strokes in the same direction. Paint the second coat in a different direction to avoid creating a tram-line effect. On wood, the final coat should follow the direction of the grain.

Gloss is rarely used on interior walls but it can be used if applied with care, although

PAINTS	SURFACES									
Primers	Wood	Metal	Plaster	Wallpaper	Brick	Stone	Concrete	Radiators	White goods	Paint
General purpose	•	•	•		•	•	•	•		•
Alkali-resistant			•		•	•	•			
Acrylic and standard wood primer	•									
Zinc phosphate primer		•								
Quick-drying metal primer		•								
Matte finishes										
Undercoat	•	•	•	•	•	•	•			
Latex flat paint			•	•	•	•	•			
New-plaster latex			•	•	•	•	•			
One-coat latex			•		•	•	•			
Flat oil paint	•	•	•	•	•	•	•	•		•
Distemper			•							
Cement paint			•		•	•	•			
Gloss/semi-gloss finishes										
Oil-based gloss	•	•	•							•
Quick-drying acrylic gloss	•									•
Bath paint		•							•	
Floor paint	•					•	•			
Eggshell/silk finishes										
Water-based eggshell/ satin finish latex	•		•	•	•	•	•			•
Oil-based eggshell	•		•							
Trade eggshell	•		•							
Radiator enamel								•	•	•
Non-slip paint	•	•			•	•	•			•
Metallic finishes										
Metallic paint	•	•								
Hammered-finish paint		•								

the surface must be flawlessly even. In the right situation, a high-gloss finish on a wall can look stunning; however, the best results will be obtained if you apply a flat or preferably eggshell finish, followed by a coat of gloss varnish. This is technically easier and you will get a superior color effect.

Metal and metallic paints

These paints are especially designed to resemble or are for use on metal. They include radiator enamel (below), which has its own special solvents; bath paint which, like radiator enamel, can be applied to "white goods" such as fridges; metallic paint colored with a metallic sheen containing copper, bronze or gold powders; and hammered-finish paint, containing aluminum, glass and resins, which needs no undercoat on metal surfaces.

Radiator enamel

This paint is usually acrylic-based and is available in satin and gloss finishes. It can be used over both latex and gloss paints, provided the paint is old and has not been rubbed down. The method of application varies between the different brands, but you will generally need to apply two coats over a compatible metal primer and use a specialist solvent for thinning and cleaning brushes.

Bath paint

An oil-based gloss intended for covering bath enamel, this is available only in a limited color range and should not be thinned down excessively. Ensure that the surface is clean, dry and grease free before applying two coats with a brush, finishing the second coat in the opposite direction to the first. This paint is slow-drying and should be left for between 16 and 24 hours before recoating.

Floor paint

This is a highly durable, usually oil-based paint suitable for use on concrete, stone, wood, composition board and tiles. Two coats are usually sufficient but you may need more, depending on the porousness of the surface you are painting. All other surfaces will need to be washed down to remove grease before application. Only a limited color range is available, and although it can be tinted with artist's oil pigments, this will weaken the paint. Floor paint should generally be used at full strength.

SURFACES
Plaster

All new plaster should be primed before you begin painting. If you intend to use an oil-based paint, first apply an alkali-resistant primer, followed by several coats of thinned flat oil or eggshell. If you wish to use latex paints for any of the broken-color techniques

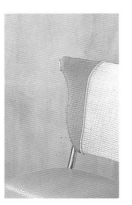

described on pages 78–101, prime the plaster by brushing on a series of thinned latex coats to seal the surface, before applying the undiluted finishing coats.

Wallpaper

It is best to avoid painting over wallpaper altogether if at all possible, but if you must, first ensure that it is well glued to the wall. You may use either oil, latex, or acrylic paints but all of these can raise the grain of the paper, so should be avoided if your aim is to achieve a smooth finish.

Interior woodwork

All interior woodwork that has been stripped, from baseboards to dining-room tables, needs to be primed with either a standard or acrylic wood primer. After that you can paint on it with oil-based flat eggshell, gloss, or acrylic paints, bearing in mind that for oil-based paints you will need to use an undercoat. All woodwork that is already covered with sound paint should be washed thoroughly with detergent or alternatively wiped down with a vinegar-and-water solution to remove any grease, and then lightly sanded if the finish is to be gloss or eggshell. You may require an undercoat if the new color is substantially different from that of the original paint.

Most interior woodwork looks best in an eggshell finish, as high-gloss paint can have a rather bleak, deadening effect. However, a gloss varnish painted over an eggshell finish will darken and add depth to the color. A wide range of broken-color

effects work well on woodwork, but ideally you should use oil-based paints as latex has little durability on wood. Water-based artist's acrylics are suitable for use on wood, but these have a different consistency to artist's oil pigments so will produce a different effect.

Metalwork

Interior metalwork should not be coated with latex paint, as this can result in rusting and will flake off very quickly. Metal should be washed down, dried and any rust removed before you begin.

Aluminum and galvanized metals, provided they are indoors, should first be painted with a zinc phosphate primer and then coated with oil-based undercoat and top coats.

Ferrous metals should be painted with a rust-inhibiting primer or a quick-drying metal primer before being painted with oil-based undercoat and top coats. (Note that these types of primer are only suitable for use on ferrous metal.) Avoid painting anything made from chrome or copper; it will be a waste of your time, as paint will not stick to either surface for any appreciable time.

Radiators

If a radiator has been coated with latex, it should not be rubbed down before you apply radiator enamels, eggshell or flat oil paints. All fixed radiators should be painted cold and in position, but always follow the manufacturer's instructions if using special enamels. Radiator brushes, with long handles and bristle heads set at right-angles, will allow you to reach between the leaves of a double radiator. Never paint over valves or fittings.

Piping

All types of pipework should be painted lengthways rather than across. The first coat on metal piping tends to be streaky, so you will need two or three coats. If you are using radiator enamel on radiator pipes, turn on the heat as soon as the paint has been applied. With other types of oil-based and metal paints, avoid turning on the heat until the paint has hardened.

Baths

The inside of a bath should be given two coats of bath enamel. The exterior can be finished in any oil-based paint suitable for metal; two or three coats will suffice.

This rose colorwash was designed to give a gentle, understated effect, so as not to overwhelm the delicate metal and glass ornaments displayed against it.
(ABOVE)

A striking use of painted parallel stripes. The mushroom color interspersed between the black and white softens the effect and prevents the floor from dominating the rest of the hallway.
(FAR LEFT)

TILES, CERAMICS, GLASS, PLASTIC AND FABRIC

The use of paint does not have to be limited to the walls, ceilings and floors of a room; it is quite possible to incorporate tiles, glass, and fabrics into your decorative scheme. Curtains, blinds, lampshades, windows, and ceramics are all suitable candidates for paint effects, provided the surface is prepared properly in advance. Specialist enamel paints are also available for decorative use on surfaces such as glass, tiles, metal jewelry and even marble.

The scope for painting on these materials is practically limitless and allows for a great deal of creativity, but it is always wise to practice your chosen designs and paint effects in advance on a piece of paper or cardboard. As a general rule, this type of decoration should enhance rather than dominate the decor of a room. Paints specifically for use on all these surfaces are available from good art supply stores.

PAINTS
Decorative acrylic enamels

Decorative acrylic enamels can be applied to glass, tiles, ceramics, jewelry, primed metal, and marble. They are water-soluble and can be mixed with specialist water-based, high-gloss varnish designed to complement them. They have a glossy finish and will not wash off when used on ceramics provided the surface has been baked. However, decorative acrylic enamels should never be used on any surface that comes into contact with food. These paints are intended to decorate an object rather than to protect it, so they are unsuitable for use on areas of heavy wear, such as tiled floors. However, if the tiles are protected with varnish and oven-heated for permanence, they can be fairly hardwearing.

Tile paints

There are excellent paints available specifically for use on tiles. Floor paints are usually necessary for painting tiles underfoot (see Interiors page 178) but oil-based ceramic paints and artist's acrylic enamels (see left) can be used for decorative work on wall or worktop tiles in kitchens, bathrooms, and fireplaces. Oil-based ceramic paints are available from art supply stores in a wide range of colors and are easy to mix.

Fabric paints

Water-soluble dyes for decorating cotton and linen fabrics, fabric paints are available in a wide color range from art supply stores. They are applied to the fabric cold and then fixed with a warm iron to "seal" the dyed pigment into the weave.

SURFACES
Tiles and ceramics

Tiles should be washed down thoroughly and dried with a soft, clean cloth before applying any sort of paint. If you are using oil-based paints, paint on a coat of tile primer. Latex and other water-based paints are unsuitable for use on tiles, as they have a tendency to

flake off the surface. Use chalk or graphite pencil rather than markers or wax crayons to draw the outline of any design. Avoid applying paint in very thick layers, as this may bubble when the tile is heated later. Paint on two coats of high-gloss varnish and allow to dry out thoroughly before baking. Pre-heat the oven to 320°F and bake for 40 minutes, keeping the area well ventilated. Heating the tiles at temperatures any higher than this may create excessive fumes.

Glass

Glass must be clean and dry before paint is applied to it. Wash down with a brand-name window cleaner or household detergent and dry with a clean, soft cloth. Neither oil-based paints nor enamels need underpainting and the former are semi-transparent on glass, but they should only be used on interior surfaces. The design can be drawn on with a soft graphite pencil, traced around with paint, or filled in with paint while the source design is laid beneath. It may be helpful to put masking tape around any straight edges of the design and, if necessary, along the glazing bars of windows.

Plastic

All plastics, from guttering to worktops, should be washed down well before painting to remove any grease and dirt. An ordinary household detergent should be sufficient. Dry with a clean, soft cloth, then apply either oil-based paints or acrylics. You do not need to use a primer on plastic.

Fabric

Many fabrics can be painted, so long as they are correctly primed. Canvas can take any kind of

paint, with the exception of water-colors (as distinct from water-based paints), as long as it has been primed using two coats of acrylic or oil-based artist's primer, allowing the surface to dry and rubbing down well between coats.

Burlap, linen, and jute all need to be primed using an acrylic primer or two thinned coats of latex. If you are using oil-based paints apply a warm, weak solution of either water- or oil-based size, available from specialist art supply stores.

A few decorative touches can be just as effective as painting an entire room. Here, a painted "rug" adds color, while the bland and featureless vinyl cupboards have been enlivened by an abstract design of circles and single brushstrokes.
(ABOVE)

A painted mat in vivid blocks of color looks stunning against a natural polished wood floor.
(FAR LEFT)

THIS CHAPTER DESCRIBES THE BASICS: HOW TO BUY
AND USE THE BEST TOOLS AND PAINTS FOR THE JOB IN
HAND FROM THE VAST RANGE AVAILABLE, AND HOW
TO PREPARE ALL KINDS OF SURFACES TO ACHIEVE THE
MOST SUCCESSFUL RESULTS.

practicalities

THE MOST COMMON PITFALLS in decorative painting stem from inadequate preparation of the surface, using the wrong type of paint, buying insufficient paint, not allowing enough time to carry out the project, and not using the right tools. These are all errors of planning and research, which can easily be avoided by spending a little time acquainting yourself with tools and materials before starting out. Once you have decided on your scheme, find out what paint will be the most durable and the easy to apply for the effect you desire. When calculating how much paint you will need, always err on the generous side rather than risking the frustrations of being unable to finish a job. Allow at least one-third more time for the work than strict calculation allows—most decorative tasks take longer than you think and the old adage of "Haste makes Waste" could have been coined to describe the key to successful decorative painting.

The variety of textures throughout this hallway—the stripped matte woodwork of the main door, the eggshell beams of the inner doors, the sheen of the floor and the flat walls—enhance the subtle color scheme.

EQUIPMENT

Brushes

Brushes are made from bristle, hair, or artificial fiber. Most brushes can be used for a variety of different tasks, but a few are designed for specific uses, such as varnishing, for which there is no substitute. Hair brushes are usually made from squirrel or ox hair and are particularly useful for fine, detailed work on smooth surfaces; however, the hairs will break up if they are used over large areas.

BRUSHES

Ordinary plasterwork and exterior masonry are normally painted with flat bristle brushes, usually 4-5in (100-125mm) wide. They should be held by the handle in the same way as a carving knife. Coarser bristle brushes are generally required for use with textured masonry paint, both inside and on exterior walls.

For painting woodwork, including furniture, you will need a smaller bristle brush than for plaster, ideally 2-3in (50-75mm) wide. This should be grasped between thumb and fingers in the same way as you would hold a pen. For awkward areas such as window frames, baseboards and molded decorations a narrower brush of 1in (25mm) or less may be necessary. Brushes cut on the diagonal are available for "cutting in" to difficult areas.

VARNISH BRUSHES

These brushes have stiff bristles which are usually either quite flat to prevent clogging, or rounded. The former are best for use on large, flat surfaces and the latter are most suitable for varnishing moldings or furniture, such as banisters and chests of drawers. You can use any varnishing brush for painting, but it is unwise to use ordinary paintbrushes for varnishing, especially those made from hair. Most paintbrushes are too thick and will lay on the varnish unevenly, while hair brushes have a tendency to molt all over the varnish.

FLOGGERS AND DRAGGERS

Floggers are fairly coarse brushes used for beating the paint surface to soften any hard lines and add texture. Draggers are similar to floggers and can be used to give parallel linear effects or for any technique which involves manipulating glazes. Both types of brush are invaluable for producing wood-graining effects.

Brushes

Floggers

STENCILING BRUSHES

Stenciling or "pounce" brushes have short, stiff bristles, ideal for working paint through stencils. They can also be used for stippling.

STIPPLERS

These are block-shaped, flat-ended brushes for stippling glazes and varnishes to produce a textured finish.

SOFTENING OR BLENDING BRUSHES

These are used dry for blending and softening the brushmarks in oil- and water-based glazes, and in techniques such as wood-graining. Badger softeners are the most effective for this purpose, but they are also very expensive. Large dusting brushes provide a cheaper alternative.

ARTIST'S BRUSHES

These come in all materials, shapes and sizes, and a good selection is indispensable for detailed painting, particularly for graining, marbling, and trompe l'oeil. The most useful shapes are those with flat bristles and square, chisel-like ends, and those with rounded bristles and arrow-shaped heads. The best-quality artist's brushes are made from sable, and give highly controlled strokes and retain paint beautifully.

PENCIL LINERS

Often used by signwriters, these are also excellent for lining and graining. Their long, tapering bristles hold more paint than other artist's brushes, making it easier to paint straight lines.

FITCHES

These are small-scale brushes with firm hoghair bristles that can be flat, rounded or pointed. They are used mainly with oil-based paints for lining, picking out moldings, spattering and other paint effects requiring detailed work.

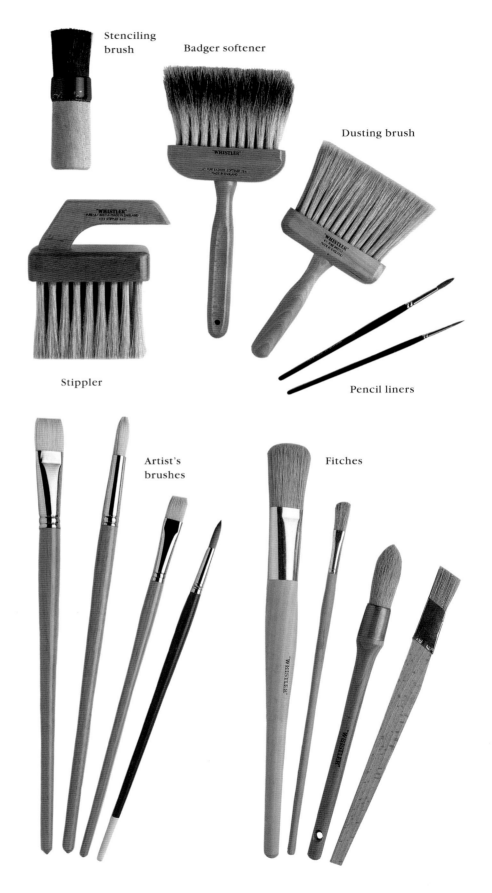

Stenciling brush

Badger softener

Dusting brush

Stippler

Pencil liners

Artist's brushes

Fitches

Rollers

The great assets of rollers are their speed and their ability to leave a textured surface. Their disadvantage is that if you work too fast, the application of paint can be superficial. Rollers are unsuitable for use with gloss paint, as the paint may peel off in long strips once dry. If you are working on a smooth surface, use a roller with a short pile; for a moderately textured surface, one with a medium pile; and for areas with rough, undulating surfaces, one with a long pile. Extension handles make it easier to paint ceilings and high walls.

Overloading a roller is a common mistake. This will cause paint to spray off the cylinder as it rotates, leaving a bubbly texture over the paint surface. Avoid this by using a sloping paint tray with ribs on the upward slope; this will prevent the roller from clogging. Pour in enough paint to fill one-third of the tray, dip the roller into the reservoir and roll it firmly over the ribs to distribute the paint, and squeeze off any surplus before application. After use, clean the roller cylinder in the appropriate solvent, then wash it in lukewarm, soapy water and hang it up to dry. If you have to stop work for a short period, place the roller in a plastic bag to keep it moist.

Paint pads and poly brushes

These are cellulose sponge rectangles mounted on a wood or plastic panel, designed for applying paint in confined areas. Unfortunately, these tend to leave only a thin, superficial layer of paint. Like rollers, avoid overloading them with paint, pressing the pad gently against the ribs of a paint tray to remove any excess before application. They can be washed in the same way as rollers and may be kept damp for short periods in plastic bags. Paint pads are unsuitable for use with gloss paints.

Paint buckets

These are plastic or metal pots into which you can decant small amounts of paint. The remaining paint can be kept covered in its can, which will prevent skin from forming on the surface. They are also useful for carrying paint cans, as they will catch any drips. When using a paint bucket, be careful not to immerse the brush in the paint right up to the handle. Dip in only the tip of the brush, removing any excess paint by pressing the bristles lightly against the sides of the bucket. Avoid wiping the brush on the rim, as this will cause a build-up of dried deposits which will drop into the paint and create lumps. At intervals, use an almost-dry brush to clean off the inside of the bucket.

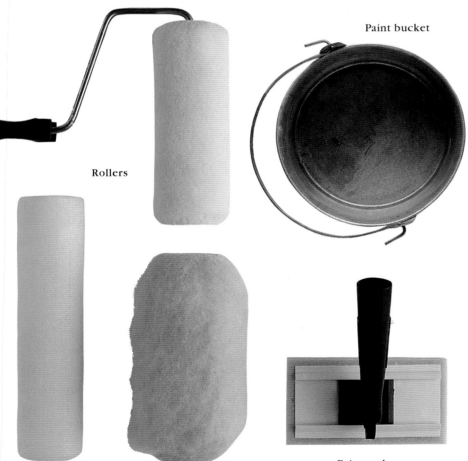

Rollers

Paint bucket

Paint pad

Looking after brushes

Buying cheap brushes is a false economy. All brushes lose a few hairs and bristles when they are new, but cheap ones shed them constantly, losing their shape in the process and spoiling the paint surface. So long as they are properly cared for, good-quality brushes will last for years.

Always wash new brushes before use to get rid of any grease and loose hairs. After washing, twirl the handle between your palms to remove excess water, rinse in paint thinner and twirl once again. Reshape the brush by hand before leaving it to dry. To break in new brushes and give any loose hairs a chance to drop, use them for preparation work rather than finishing coats.

CLEANING BRUSHES

Brushes used for oil-based paint should be cleaned in paint thinner, then washed in lukewarm, soapy water, rinsed, reshaped and hung up by the handle to dry. Never leave damp brushes pointing upwards: any remaining paint will drizzle down to the roots, solidify, and cause the hairs or bristles to separate.

To remove water-based paint, brushes should be first rinsed in cold water, then washed in warm, soapy water, rinsed, reshaped, and hung up to dry.

Store brushes flat once they are fully dry. If your house is prone to attack by moths, pack some mothballs in with the brushes.

If you are using oil-based paint, brushes can be stored temporarily overnight by suspending them in jar containing a 1:1 mixture of raw linseed oil and paint thinner. To make this easier, drill a small hole at the top of each handle and insert a piece of wire from which to hang each brush. Cover the container to keep out air and dust. Before re-using, rinse brushes in paint thinner and twirl them dry. Latex brushes can be kept moist for short intervals by placing them inside a plastic bag.

Paint removers

BURNERS

Burning off old paint is often a quicker process than using chemical strippers, especially when removing a great many layers of paint; however, stonework or large areas of plaster can easily be cracked unless burning is carried out with care. Burners are cleaner than chemical strippers, but you should bear in mind that old lead-based paint can emit toxic fumes, and oil-based paint on wood can catch fire, so always refer to the manufacturer's guidelines for use before starting work.

Blowtorches usually consist of adjustable nozzles attached to a gas cylinder, allowing you to alter the shape and intensity of the flame. The flame is hotter than that of blowlamps and hot-air blowers, and it will not blow out in a draught.

Blowlamps are often considered quaint today, as more powerful alternatives are now available. Usually powered by paraffin or gas, blowlamps have a cooler flame than blowtorches. They also have a tendency to blow out or flare, and need frequent refueling. If you hold the flame too close to the surface, you risk setting fire to the paint. Their main advantage is that they are cheap to use over small areas.

Hot-air blowers blow air along a flexible hose and over a heater, which has a variable control and insulated hand piece. They are safer to use than burners incorporating a naked flame and can be used on any surface, although they can be slow to shift paint on stone. While blowtorches are quicker, you are less likely to scorch wood with hot-air blowers and they are also highly effective on detailed moldings.

Electric strippers come in a variety of sizes and are very useful for areas of detailed work, such as the turnings of chair legs, but the nozzles of the smaller ones are useless over a larger area.

CHEMICAL STRIPPERS

These are used to remove paint from wood, plaster, tiles, or metal without damaging the surface. Avoid skin contact with all strippers by wearing gloves and protective clothing. Strippers can damage fabric and leather, so be careful not to let them drip onto upholstery or shoes. There are two kinds of strippers: alkaline and alcohol.

Alkaline strippers are the faster and more powerful of the two types, and are most commonly used by professional decorators. They are highly effective, softening the paint so that it blisters and becomes malleable and easy to scrape off. However, they may give wood grain a raised appearance and can be more difficult to wash off than other paint removers. These strippers are also toxic if inhaled, so always work in a well-ventilated area and wear a protective mask and gloves.

Alcohol strippers are less potent than alkaline strippers and are therefore safer for use in domestic surroundings; however, the same safety precautions still apply. Alcohol strippers are easier to wash off than alkaline types and some can be used on plastics.

Edged tools

SCRAPERS

Broad- and narrow-bladed, pliable scrapers are the best stripping tools for flat areas of wood and plaster. The blade should be held almost flat against the surface to avoid inflicting damage.

Scrapers can also be used to mask or shield areas from paint, by holding the blade over the surface you wish to protect while painting along a straight edge such as a baseboard.

SHAVE HOOKS

These are either triangular-headed, with the head set at right-angles to the shaft, or combination hooks with curved edges. The former are useful for cutting into corners, while the latter are invaluable for cleaning the curved edges of moldings.

FLAT-HEADED SCREWDRIVERS

These are excellent for levering the lids off paint cans, but be sure to work around the lid rather than pulling hard at one spot, which will either buckle the lid or cause it to spring open.

PALETTE KNIVES

These pliable steel blades are used by artists for mixing paint and varnish. Those shaped like a long, thin spatula are specially made for mixing pigment into oil-based paint. Trowel-shaped palette knives can be used for painting.

Tools for measuring and marking out

LEVEL

This is a wooden or metal rod with an alcohol-filled phial in the center, and is used for finding a true horizontal. When the bubble of liquid is positioned in the center of the phial, the surface is exactly level.

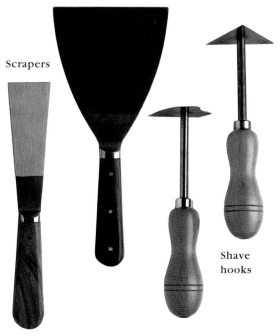

Palette knives

Scrapers

Shave hooks

Plumbline   Levels

Measuring tape

PLUMBLINE

This is a cord with a lead weight at the bottom which is used to reveal a true vertical. It is essential where any vertical patterning or marking out is required.

MEASURING TAPE

This is useful for measuring out grids and, because it does not tear or knot and remains relatively taut, it can be hooked around an object and used by one person.

STEEL RULER

This is ideal for use as a cutting edge, as it is less prone to damage than a wooden ruler.

STRAIGHT-EDGE

This can be any stiff, straight-edged object with an undulation-free surface. It is generally used as a guide when marking out or painting straight lines.

Abrasive materials

STEEL WOOL

This comes in many grades from very fine to coarse, and resembles a bundle of gray hair. It may be used dry or with water and oil, and is highly effective for rubbing down paintwork and giving a "key" to smooth surfaces such as galvanized steel or aluminum, as well as for preparing surfaces for oil-based paint. Steel wool can also be used with paint thinner to remove rust.

BRONZE WOOL

This serves the same purpose as steel wool but is used for preparing surfaces for water-based paints: steel wool sometimes sheds particles, which become embedded and may cause rust beneath latex paints.

SANDPAPER

This is primarily intended for smoothing wood and removing dry paint. It comes in many grades from very fine (00) to rough, but you should avoid using the coarser grades on plastic or when smoothing paintwork as they may leave gashes. Use sandpaper in a circular motion whenever possible. Aluminum oxide sandpaper is specifically designed for use on metal.

WET-AND-DRY PAPER

Like black sandpaper with a fabric backing, this is ideal for rubbing down fillers and plaster. It can be used either dry or dampened: wetting the surfaces decreases the risk of gashing. Self-lubricating paper, which should be used slightly damp, is also available. Use 400 and 600 only on furniture.

DISC SANDING

All types of sandpaper can be used on the disc sanding attachment of an electric drill. This can be highly effective and fast for smoothing rough wood and removing dry paint, but it should never be used on a fragile surface.

Abrasive materials.
From top to bottom:
Steel wool
Coarse and fine
sandpaper
Coarse, medium and
fine wet-and-dry paper
Coarse and fine
finishing paper.

Ladders and scaffolds

Both ladders and scaffolds are cheap to rent and you will work more quickly, efficiently, and safely if you can reach easily across an area. Using makeshift structures can be very dangerous and should be avoided.

STEPLADDERS

Stepladders, among the most stable of structures, are essential for work indoors. Most metal stepladders have folding alloy bracing struts between their sections and these should always be locked in place. Old wooden ladders often have a rope between the sections and you should always check that this is secure and unworn. Choose a ladder with wide, comfortable treads. A platform at the top is useful for taking paint trays and cans. If you have two stepladders you can place two boards between them, tying them across, one step down from the top, to form a walkway.

EXTENSION OR STRAIGHT LADDERS

These are available in both wood and alloy, but the former should have metal reinforcers on their rungs. On an extension ladder the rungs of the overlapping sections should always align, otherwise the gaps between the rungs may be too small for you to insert your foot properly. Choose an extension ladder with a rope and pulley, as this will enable you to extend it easily yourself, and one which has an automatic latch that locks the extension in position.

DUAL OR MULTI-PURPOSE LADDERS

These can be used either as straight ladders or hinged down to form the triangular shape of a stepladder.

USING LADDERS OUTSIDE

When working on hard surfaces, such as concrete, use anti-slip end caps on the feet of the ladder and steady the base with a sandbag or plastic bag filled with earth.

When you extend a ladder, the end of each section should overlap by at least one-quarter of its length. Never lean a ladder against the glazing bars of a window, as it may break the bars and smash the glass. Gutters and drainpipes should also be avoided, as they can easily give way. To estimate the length of ladder necessary to paint a house exterior, add together the ceiling heights of the house, plus 3ft 3in (1m) to allow for the angle and access to a platform.

Never climb higher than four rungs from the top of a ladder, as you will be unable to balance properly without adequate hand holds, and keep both feet on the same rung with your hips centered between the rungs. Always climb down and move a ladder along rather than lean out precariously to the side. If the ground is wet, place an old doormat or sacking at the foot of the ladder to wipe slippery material from the soles of your shoes before you climb up.

USING LADDERS INSIDE

Stepladders can topple over if you lean out from them to the side. On uneven floors you may need to clamp a strut to each side which extends diagonally outwards to the floor.

SCAFFOLDS

Scaffold platforms are by far the easiest means of painting the outside of a building. There are two main types of scaffolding: tower and pipe girder. The latter is best left to professional contractors, as unless you are fully familiar with its use you may run into legal difficulties in the event of an accident.

Tower scaffolds fit together in sections to form a hollow tower and can usually be hired. They are available up to a maximum of 30ft (9m), but "outriggers" or diagonal stabilizers are necessary once they are over three frame sections high. Some models are on castors, allowing you to wheel them around. These should always be locked before climbing onto the scaffold.

Handling and erecting ladders

Wooden or alloy extension ladders can be heavy and unwieldy objects, so should always be handled with care. Never carry a ladder over your shoulder. To pick up a ladder, bend your knees slightly, then lean it back vertically against your shoulder. Grip one of the rungs at head height with one hand, grip another lower down with the other, and then straighten your knees.

Protective coverings

PLASTIC SHEETING

Cheap, transparent and available in a variety of weights, plastic sheeting is useful for masking windows while working around them. The lightest can be flimsy, but they are extremely pliable and can be stuffed into corners and crevices. The heavier weights are more suitable for floors and exterior use.

FABRIC DROP CLOTHS

These are useful for protecting furniture from paint, but they should not be used when stripping off paint with a burner unless first soaked thoroughly in water.

RUBBER GLOVES

Always wear rubber gloves when using chemicals such as strippers and solvents. If your skin is particularly sensitive you should also wear them when painting—high-quality, concentrated paints such as flat oil paints can cause a skin reaction.

GOGGLES AND MASKS

If you are painting above your head, wearing a pair of goggles, or even old sunglasses, will help to keep paint out of your eyes. If you are stripping paint in this position, eye protection is essential. Few modern paints sold for decorating purposes are toxic, but paint stripping and sanding, especially with disc sanders and a naked flame, can cause fumes and paint dust. You should always wear a mask for these jobs, especially if you are stripping off old, lead-based paint. If there are many layers of paint and the surface is sound, it is always better to work over the surface rather than disturbing old paint.

SAFETY CHECK LIST

Using oil- and water-based paints and chemical strippers
- Ensure good ventilation while applying the finish and when it is drying.
- Do not smoke in the area.
- Wear a respirator, not just a mask, if you suffer from a breathing disorder.
- Wear gloves or a brand-name barrier cream if you have sensitive skin.
- Always wear gloves when using a chemical stripper.
- Cover any flooring or furniture with damp drop cloths.
- If you get paint in your eyes, wash them with a great deal of water, with the eyelids held open; if you experience any further problems, see a doctor immediately.
- Do not use paint thinners to remove paint from your skin. Use a brand-name skin cleaner, or wash off paint with warm, soapy water.
- Keep paint, solvents or any chemicals out of children's reach. If they swallow them, do not try to induce vomiting, and call medical help immediately.

Using blowtorches
- Keep a bucket of water nearby.
- Wear a mask and gloves, or a respirator if you have a breathing disorder.
- If working overhead, cover your face with a damp cloth and wear goggles or clear glasses.
- Cover the floor beneath the work with a drop cloth soaked in water.
- Keep the area well ventilated but free from strong drafts.
- Always extinguish the flame when you stop work.

Painting outside
- Contain any paint spillages with earth or sand and do not allow paint to enter a drain.
- Cover any paths and shrubs below the painting work with ground sheets.
- Do not leave chemicals in black plastic bags in sunlight or near a heat source, as they can combust.

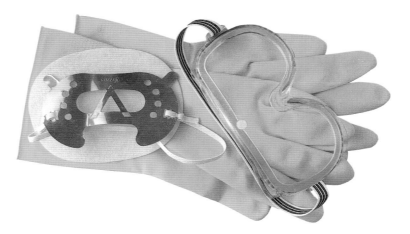

Buying paint

Paint designed for interior or exterior decoration is generally sold by shops often bearing the brand name of the manufacturer. Trade suppliers stock high-quality paints and tools for the same purpose, but the latter often require a little more expertise to apply them to a high standard. Art supply stores sell paints and pigments specifically designed for use by artists, not decorators, but many of their products are necessary to produce some of the more sophisticated paint effects.

Many decorative paint manufacturers show a huge range of colors on their charts, which are made by blending the main tints and tones of their collection. These colors are usually mixed mechanically on the spot at the customer's request from a standard balance of ingredients.

Most major paint manufacturers offer seasonal collections of colors (in the same way as the fashion industry) which may, for example, be available in their satin latex or exterior masonry paint range, and after a year or so specific shades may be discontinued. It is therefore unwise to assume that a shade which you used some time ago will continue to be available years later and you should check, although you may be able to get a reasonably close match mixed if you keep a sample of the original color.

In recent years "historical" color ranges have appeared, which reproduce the general color types common in previous centuries. These are often well researched, although they do not purport to be exact reproductions of bygone paint shades, merely very similar to those originally used. They tend to have names like "Heritage" colors.

It can be very frustrating to be forced into buying gallons of paint when all you need is a sample to test the color. Most reputable paint suppliers will produce small test amounts of a color, especially if it is one of those which you have requested to be mixed; the minimum amount is generally about 18fl oz (500ml), as the filler in the paint means the automatic mixers cannot color-balance smaller amounts.

STORAGE

Most good-quality commercial decorating paint will last for many years if kept airtight in a sealed metal can. Once opened, however, a paint's shelf life is immediately reduced. All paint varies, but oil-based types generally form a skin if left in a partly empty, closed can, while the pigment and solvent may separate beneath. Break and remove the skin, then decant the paint and stir it well or strain through a cheescloth. Water-based paints left in similar situations tend to solidify. Paint left in plastic containers will quickly coagulate or evaporate. All paint should be kept in a cool place and out of direct sunlight.

Artist's pigments behave quite differently. Oil-based paints in lead tubes will last a lifetime, provided that the tube is undamaged and the cap secure, and acrylics similarly, provided that the cap is not loose, otherwise the paint will gradually solidify throughout the tube.

All paint manufacturers produce color range samples to help with your selection of shade and finish: those shown here are from a range of traditional paint colors. (BELOW)

PAINTS — PAINT COVERAGE AND DRYING TIMES

	AVERAGE COVERAGE sq yd per gallon	THINNERS/SOLVENTS Paint thinner	Water	NUMBER OF COATS	DRYING TIME (hours) Touch dry	Recoatable
Matte finishes						
Flat latex	36–60		•	2	1–2	4
New-plaster latex	44		•	1–2	1–2	4
One-coat latex	32		•	1	3–4	
Flat oil paint	60–64	•		1–2	2–4	16–18
Distemper	variable		•	1	1–2	
Limewash	variable		•	1–2	1–2	
Cement paint	4–24		•	2	1–2	24
Water-based masonry paint	16–40		•	2	1–2	4–6
Oil-based masonry paint	36–64	•		2	4–6	16
Reinforced masonry paint	12–26	•	•	1–2	2–3	24
Asphaltum	36–60	•	•	1–3	1–2	6–24
Textured paint	8–12		•	1	24	
Water-based exterior latex	36–48		•	2	1–2	4
Gloss/semi-gloss finishes						
Oil-based gloss	60–64	•		2–3	2–4	16–18
Quick-drying acrylic gloss	40		•	1–2	1	1–2
Bath paint	52–56	•		2	6–10	16–24
Floor paint	20–40	•	•	2	2–3	3–16
Eggshell/silk finishes						
Water-based eggshell/ satin finish latex	36–48		•	2	1–2	4
Oil-based eggshell	60–64	•		1–2	2–4	16–18
Trade eggshell	60–64	•		1–2	2–4	16–18
Radiator enamel	52	Specialist solvents		1–2	2–6	7–14
Non-slip paint	12–20	•		1	2–4	
Metallic finishes						
Metallic paint	40–56	•		1–2	4	8
Hammered-finish paint	12–20	Specialist solvents		1–2	0.5	1–3

PREPARING SURFACES

You can paint on any primed wall in good condition, whether new plaster (you will need to wait for up to six months after plastering to allow the water content to come to the surface), old plaster, sealed woodwork, sound varnish, primed fabric, painted or scoured metal, lining paper, the backing paper of vinyls, or tiles and glass. However, it is inadvisable to paint on crumbling or unsealed plaster, peeling paint, polyurethane varnish and old wallpaper, and you should never paint on old distemper, whiting, limewash, unsealed wood, felt or unprepared metal.

Plaster

OLD PLASTER

If plaster has been painted and is in good condition, it needs only to be washed down with warm, soapy water, rinsed and left to dry, regardless of the type of paint you intend to apply. Use a mild water-and-vinegar solution to remove any grease. Wax can be rubbed off using an artist's eraser. The plaster will not require sealing, but it may need an undercoat to hide its previous color before you apply new top coats.

If the paint on the plaster has bubbled, wrinkled or cracked, it will have to be stripped. However, if the paint is only defective in one or two places, you can simply remove these patches and sand down the edges of the stripped areas until they are flush with the rest of the paintwork. Paint can often be scraped off with a scraper, keeping the blade flat to prevent it from digging into the plaster, but you can also use chemical strippers or burn it off.

CHEMICAL STRIPPERS

Chemicals can be used to remove latex from plaster, although this is rarely necessary, and they also work well on oil-based paints. The job cannot be rushed. Wearing rubber gloves, brush on the stripper with an old, wide-bristled brush and leave it to work for at least 30 minutes or as advised by the manufacturer. Paste-type strippers should always be laid on in one direction only and liquid types benefit from several applications, always keeping the surface wet. For both types, apply the first coat and wait for the paint surface to soften before adding a second, thick coat. Chemical strippers can take anywhere from two hours to two days to eat through a heavy build-up of paint, but patience always pays off and the paint will finally peel off easily, leaving the surface beneath bare and unscarred.

When all the paint has been removed, wash down the plaster with water or paint thinner, whichever is appropriate to the stripper, and leave to dry. Newly stripped plaster is highly absorbent, so you will need to use a primer before painting.

BURNERS

Heat removes oil-based paint from wood more quickly than chemicals, but it rarely works faster on plaster unless the paint is very thick. Plaster and stonework can easily crack if overheated. When using a blow-torch, blowlamp or hot-air blower, always start at the base of a wall, because heat rises and will soften the paint above you, making your task progressively easier. Move the flame or blower constantly, aiming to heat about 1sq ft (30sq cm) at a time. Once paint has been heated and left to dry again, it will be even harder to remove. The paint should blister rather than turning into a gluey mess. As you move the heat upwards, use the scraper behind it, keeping the blade as flat as you can and moving it from side to side. Always cover floors and furniture, and follow the safety precautions on page 191.

REMOVING DISTEMPER, LIMEWASH AND WHITING

These finishes all leave a powdery trace on the fingers when touched and should be removed before overpainting, because, with the exception of properly applied limewash, they will be carried off by the new paint. Scrub the surface with a dry brush to remove any loose flakes, then soak it thoroughly with warm water, rubbing vigorously with the stiffest brush you can find. Change the water each time it becomes milky and, once you have removed all the distemper, rinse the area with clean water and swab it dry with a sponge or soft cloth. Leave the wall to dry thoroughly before applying primer, sealer or paint, otherwise damp will gather beneath the finish.

PREPARING A STRIPPED WALL

Defects in plaster should be filled using any composition or powder filler available from decorating shops. Fillers tend to be very pale, but can be tinted to blend in with your final paint color. Once the filled patch is dry, sand it down using very fine sandpaper in a gentle circular motion until it is flush with the surrounding surface.

If you intend to apply water-based paint, give the whole wall a coat of primer or an extra coat of latex, otherwise the treated area will show up when dry. If you are using

a gloss or oil-based eggshell, touch up the filled area with an oil-based paint diluted 1:1 with paint thinner. Once it is dry, sand down the edges of the old paint, fill and retouch it again, allow it to dry, and then apply the first coat of the new finish.

PREPARING NEW PLASTER

In theory, new plaster should be silky smooth and absolutely level; however, it often has a few hair-line cracks and bubbles. The latter can be smoothed by sliding a broad, flat scraper horizontally across the surface, being careful not to tilt the blade more than a few degrees to avoid digging into the new plaster. Never sand new plaster, as it will leave gashes which will show up through layers of paint.

If you want to apply oil-based paint, first apply an alkali-resistant primer. This will prevent not only any dampness from creating a piebald effect, but also the bubbling and cracking caused by salts and acids coming to the surface. Allow this to dry before painting on a coat of undercoat.

If you are using water-based paint, salts and acids can be left to bleed through the plaster and then brushed off as a fluffy ash. Give the surface a "mist" or "fog" coat of 1:1 paint to water to seal it. This will also reveal any cracks, which can be filled with vinyl-based fillers. Allow the filler to dry, then smooth it down with very fine sandpaper once you have sealed the surface around it. Touch it up with the 1:1 paint-and-water mixture. Repeat this process if any cracks re-open, before applying the finishing coats.

Wood

CHEMICAL STRIPPERS

These are ideal for removing paint from turnings and recesses in wooden furniture and wall moldings. Apply the chemicals as for plaster (see page 194) and, when the

Tack-cloths

These are ideal for cleaning grit and dust from stripped wood. Make one by soaking a white lint-free cloth (such as an old shirt) in warm water, wringing it out and spreading it onto a non-porous surface. Scatter turpentine across the surface, squeeze it out so that this is evenly distributed through the fibres, then open up the cloth and sprinkle over a large spoonful of boat varnish. Wring out the cloth once again and hang it up for 40 minutes. Fold up the cloth into a pad and it is ready to use. If stored in an airtight container the cloth will remain tacky for many months and can simply be retreated when it begins to dry out. Always shake it out after use, or you will simply recycle the grit next time you use it.

paint has softened, remove it using a small shave hook scraper, an old toothbrush, a skewer or steel wool. Across larger areas, use a scraper. Always work from the top downwards to prevent sticky paint from dropping onto the stripped wood, and work in the direction of the grain. When you have finished, wash down the surface thoroughly with a sponge or hose.

BURNERS

As for plaster, work from the base upwards and keep the heat source moving over an area of 1sq ft (30sq cm) at a time. The blade should follow the flame upwards, but always work in the direction of the grain, never across it. Always cover floors and furniture, and follow the safety precautions on page 191.

REMOVING LACQUER

Never use heat for removing lacquer. Special lacquer removers, usually requiring about three applications, can be painted on with a brush. A cabinetmaker's scraper is the ideal tool for removing softened lacquer, followed by a firm sponge to wipe down the surface. Lacquer removers vary in their use, so always read the manufacturer's instructions.

REMOVING VARNISH AND WAX

The quickest way to remove varnish, dirt and wax is to apply a chemical paint and varnish remover. Follow the method described for removing paint (see pages 196–7) using a cabinetmaker's steel scraper. Polyurethane varnish can be taken off with chemical paint remover, but you should never use lacquer or shellac removers.

PREPARING NEW OR NEWLY STRIPPED WOOD

Always sand new wood with fine sandpaper or steel wool to remove fibrous splinters and provide a key for the paint. Soft woods,

especially pine, tend to have resinous knots which can bleed into paint. These can be chiseled out, or knocked out of a board using a chisel and wooden mallet. Fill the hole with a wood filler, sand it flat when dry and prime it. Alternatively, splice in a piece of wood or cover knots with aluminum primer or two thin coats of knotting—a solution of pure shellac—diluting it with methylated spirit and spreading the solution about 1in (2.5cm) beyond the knots.

Aluminum primers are most effective on doors and window frames, especially where wood abuts brickwork and stone, and they are preferable on frames made from hardwoods. On other woods and most furniture, you can use a good lead-free primer. Combined primer undercoats are often most convenient. For use on highly absorbent softwoods, the primer should be diluted with paint thinner to seal the wood. This is not necessary for hardwoods.

If there are still traces of paint on stripped wood, dampen the wood and rub it down with wet-and-dry paper. Leave it to dry, and if the grain swells, smooth it down again with sandpaper before priming. Alternatively, mix 1:3 parts linseed oil to paint thinner and rub it in with self-lubricating paper. Then wash the wood with paint thinner using a lint-free cloth.

Wallpaper

PREPARING WALLPAPER FOR PAINTING

Wallpaper must be very firmly glued to the wall if you intend to paint over it, as paint is surprisingly heavy and may cause the paper to sag or fall off. The dyes in older papers can bleed into paint, especially reds and mauves, and the paint will accentuate any joints and tears. It is almost always simpler to strip off old wallpaper completely, but if you do want to paint over it, never paint size onto old wallpaper in an attempt to seal and stiffen it as the paper will swell, then shrink, trapping hundreds of air bubbles underneath, before coming away from the wall when the paint dries. Painting water-thinned, water-based paint over wallpaper will give the same results. To prevent this happening, try priming the paper, then give it a coat of thinned oil-based paint. However, this may raise the grain of the wallpaper, so is not advisable unless you are going to apply a textured finish. If dye from the wallpaper bleeds into this, give the whole lot a coat of knotting—a solution of pure shellac—diluted with methylated spirits. Finally, cross-line the walls: that is, put on lining paper horizontally.

REMOVING WALLPAPER

Wallpaper, especially pre-pasted or thickly embossed types, can sometimes be stripped off dry using a knife or scraper. It may also pull away easily if the wall is very damp, or the plaster is crumbly or has been heated. Work from the bottom up, inserting a knife or scraper under a lower corner and sliding it gently upwards; if you start from the top, the paper will fall onto you as you work.

If you have difficulties removing paper in this way, the most effective and least messy method is to soak the walls with very hot water using a large, flat brush. Do this several times and work from the top, allowing the water to run down the walls. Then strip off the paper using a large, flat scraper. This time, work downwards and use horizontal strokes. Paper comes away quickest like this because the resistance of the width of the roll is naturally less than that of its length.

STEAMING OFF WALLPAPER

A thick build-up of many layers of wallpaper is usually easiest to remove using steam. It may be worth buying or renting a steam stripper, especially if you are removing paper from a large area. These have a perforated plate at the end of a long hose, which is held against the paper for about 30 seconds at a time: any longer and the steam may cause the plaster to bulge. The wallpaper can then be removed by running a scraper or knife upwards and across the wall as before. Thick textured or embossed papers may need scrubbing with a sharp brush to make them fall away.

The only wallpaper known to resist a steam stripper is Victorian varnished paper. You can try scoring it with a blade, then holding the plate or nozzle of the stripper against the crack before inserting a scraper, but if this fails you will have to cover it with new paint or paper. Modern washable papers are also difficult to remove, as they were designed to resist steam and are thin and filmy. However, you should be able to remove them by soaking with hot water and scoring them as above, before using the steam stripper.

After removing wallpaper, wash the wall thoroughly to remove any old paste or size. Leave until completely dry, then rub it down with sandpaper, dust it off and apply a suitable primer.

Metal

Apart from wrought iron, most metals are difficult to paint without careful preparation, particularly chrome, copper, galvanized steel and aluminum.

WROUGHT IRON

This is normally used for gates, decorative ironwork and garden furniture. Paints specifically designed for use on wrought iron are widely available, although the color range is rather restricted. All gloss paints can be used on wrought iron, but they should always be applied over a suitable undercoat or primer.

STEEL AND GALVANIZED STEEL

Sound, unrusted steel should be washed with paint thinner and then painted with a metal primer. Galvanized metals should be cleaned with a mordant solution and then primed with either galvanized, metal or acrylic primer. Both kinds of steel can then be painted with oil-based or enamel paints.

RADIATORS

Radiators are usually painted with enamel. If the original paint has chipped or rusted it can be stripped off using chemicals. Never use heat to strip a radiator. Prime the surface with a proprietary metal primer. Radiator paints are available and eggshell and flat oil paints are also suitable, but gloss paints should be avoided as they are not very efficient conductors of heat. Water-based paints should never be used on radiators.

ALUMINUM

Aluminum is not normally painted, but it can be coated with high-quality model-maker's enamels or motor vehicle spray enamels available from good-quality hardware stores, and motor industry suppliers. Ensure that the metal is clean, dry and grease free before application.

COPPER AND CHROME

Copper and chrome are best left unpainted, as paint tends to flake off when heated. However, if you must paint them, use a zinc chromate primer followed by gloss paint. It will not last very long, but will survive longer than other methods.

Tiles

Unpainted tiles need only be washed down with detergent to remove any grease, then rinsed with a 1:1 mixture of water and vinegar and left to dry. To clean paint from tiles, use a chemical stripper (see page 188). Never burn paint off tiles as they will crack.

Removing rust from metal

Rust should always be removed before painting. Chemical rust removers are quite sufficient for dealing with light rust, but they in turn must be cleaned off thoroughly or they will prevent the paint from adhering. Heavier rust is much more laborious to remove. Wear a heavy pair of gloves and use a scraper, followed by a brush and steel wool, and keep going until the metal is clean and bare.

Glass

Glass should always be washed with a brand-name window cleaner before painting, and the surface can be scraped with a flat, blunt instrument such as a window scraper or a razor blade. Dry the glass with a soft cloth.

Fabrics

BURLAP, LINEN AND JUTE

You can paint on all of these fabrics so long as they are stretched taut. It is best to prime them first, using an acrylic primer or two thinned coats of latex. If you are using oil-based paints, apply a warm, weak solution of size, available from an art supply store. This will penetrate the fabric weave and prevent it from becoming brittle. When it dries, size lightens in color. Apply a primer before the finishing coat.

CANVAS

New canvas should be primed and stretched onto a frame or "stretcher." This should have enough lateral strength to resist the powerful pull of the canvas, and if it is larger than 3 x 4ft (90 x 120cm) it will need at least one cross-piece at the center. The canvas should be about 3in (7.5cm) larger all the way round than the frame. Lay the frame onto the canvas, fold the canvas around the edges, and then tack or staple it into place. Work on all sides simultaneously, starting from the center of each side and working out to the corners, which should be tucked in like a bed sheet. The canvas should be taut, but not too tight.

Using a wide brush, coat the canvas with acrylic or oil-based artist's primer, working backwards and forwards, without scrubbing, so that the primer fills the small holes in the weave. Allow to dry for about 24 hours, by which time the canvas should be drumskin taut. Rub it down with fine sandpaper using a circular motion. Apply a second coat of primer and rub it down again before painting.

Sequence for painting surfaces

INTERIORS

The best order in which to paint a room is to start with the ceiling, followed by the walls, and finally the woodwork. When painting ceilings and walls, begin with the points at which the walls meet each other or the ceiling and use the tip of your brush.

CEILINGS

Always start at the window side and work across the ceiling in 2ft (60cm) strips running parallel to the window, not leading towards it. Cover areas about 2ft (60cm) square at a time, spreading the paint evenly with broad strokes.

Finally, lay off (make your finishing strokes) towards the light. Try to avoid overlapping the strips while you are brushing on the paint. As you paint each strip, cross-brush and lay off towards the light to blend the two wet edges. Work steadily and briskly without rushing.

WALLS

If you are left handed, start at the top left-hand corner; if right, at the top right-hand corner. Work from top to bottom in horizontal 2ft (60cm) strips running parallel to the ceiling, cross-brushing each strip into the next and laying off with a light downward stroke.

WOODWORK

When painting woodwork, start with the window frames, followed by the picture rail, dado rail, doors, mantelpiece and finally the baseboard. In this way, those areas which are most likely to have dirt on them will be painted last.

STAIRCASES

On staircases, always start with the banisters, taking care not to let the paint drip down the edges of moldings. Next paint the treads and risers, working your way down from the top of the staircase. If you know you will have to use the staircase before the paint has had a chance to dry, paint all the risers but leave alternate treads unpainted, to allow you to go up and down the stairs two at a time. Paint the remaining treads the following day.

DOORS

To paint doors, start with any inner panels, followed by the top, inner and outer edges, and finish with the lower edge and door frame.

WINDOWS

Start with the outside edges, followed by the inner and flanking window bars, then paint the upper and lower frames, and finish with the windowsill.

EXTERIORS

The most practical order in which to paint the exterior of a building is to start with the roof, followed by the walls, and then finally the woodwork. Roof areas include the weatherboard beneath the guttering, because although this is often wooden, painting it before the walls ensures that any paint which drips onto the wall can then be overpainted.

Most exterior wall paint tends to be thick and is often applied over textured surfaces, so overlapping paint strokes will be less apparent than on an interior wall. If, however, the wall is smooth and the paint has been tinted or thinned, it is best to work in horizontal bands as for interior walls, starting from the top and taking the joints between the main paint areas to the edges of the windows.

The sequence for painting exterior windows and doors is the same as for interiors. Paint windows on the upper floors first, working down the building, and finishing with the doors. Fences and any woodwork at the lowest level should be painted last.

TINTING AND MAKING PAINTS, VARNISHES AND GLAZES

Tinting means adding pigment to a paint, varnish or glaze to alter its color. Pigments are available either in a tube or as a powder, and can be oil-based (artist's oil pigments) or water-based (artist's acrylics and gouaches) (see Directory of Paints and Surfaces, pages 160–81). Paints can also be used as a tinting agent.

DECORATING PAINT

Most commercial decorating paints are mixed ready for application and contain a high percentage of filler. Therefore, adding pigment to most of these paints at a ratio of more than 1:8 pigment to paint may cause them to set. Always test a small sample of tinted paint before mixing the full amount, because the color will alter slightly when dry. Oil-based paint should be tinted with artist's oil pigments, and water-based paint with artist's acrylic (water-based) pigments.

OIL-BASED VARNISH

Many varnishes claim to be colorless, but most oil-based varnishes have a pale amber tone, which "mellows" many surfaces and adds to the visual depth of the color beneath. Yellow and brown pigments are often added to heighten this effect. However, extra-pale oil-based varnishes are available if you want a finish with clear blue or cool tones. Tint oil-based varnish using artist's oil pigments or universal tints. Decant the varnish into a paint tray or paint bucket and use a palette knife to stir in the colorant, adding only a little at a time as it disperses rapidly. Check that the pigment is dispersed before application, as undissolved granules can cause streaking.

ACRYLIC VARNISH

Acrylic varnish is generally cloudy in its concentrated form but dries to a colorless film. However, if applied too thickly it has a chalky quality and gives a "pearly" finish to paler colors. It also has a cooling effect on intense color. It can be tinted with water-based pigments such as acrylics, gouaches and watercolors or universal tints, but the pigment must be thoroughly dispersed before application. Because acrylic varnish is very quick drying, it is important to tint a sufficient quantity to cover the intended area, as it will be difficult to blend a second mix into the first batch. If you run out of varnish before you finish, you will have to wash off the first covering and start again.

POLYURETHANE VARNISH

Polyurethane varnish is oil-based and is available in both clear and ready-tinted forms. However, it can be tinted with artist's oil pigments in the same way as oil-based varnish.

OIL-BASED GLAZE

Oil-based glaze is usually tinted with artist's oil pigments. The higher the ratio of glaze to pigment, the more transparent the finish. It can also be tinted with decorating paint for a slightly opaque finish.

ACRYLIC SCUMBLE GLAZE

Acrylic scumble glaze is tinted with artist's acrylics or latex paints for an opaque effect. Whereas oil-based scumble has a slight yellow tone, acrylics have a faint white, powdery element and so successive layers may appear slightly "hazy."

PAINT GLAZES

Paint glazes are paints thinned either with paint thinner or water and applied without the addition of varnish or glaze. These are normally applied over a coat of unthinned paint to enhance or adjust the color.

JAPAN DRYERS

These can be added to oil-based glazes or paints to speed up the drying time. Follow the manufacturer's instructions with care, as exceeding the recommended amount of dryer can lead to the deterioration of the paint or glaze.

Making paint

CLAIRCOLLE DISTEMPER

Often known as "soft distemper" because of its powdery texture, this is the most commonly used type of distemper. You will need 7lb (3kg) of whiting (powdered chalk) and rabbit-skin glue, both of which are available from art supply stores. Half fill a bucket with cold water. Pour in the whiting until it forms a peak above the surface and leave to soak overnight. The next day, pour off a little of the water, then stir well until you have a smooth paste. Now mix in about 1 part hot rabbit-skin glue to 9 parts paste. The distemper should be about the same consistency as standard latex paint. To tint the distemper, dissolve a little powder pigment in water and mix in thoroughly to prevent streaking.

CASEIN (MILK-BASED) DISTEMPER

Casein powder is available from specialist art supply stores. Mix 1:4 parts casein powder to water in a basin, putting in the casein first and adding the water slowly, stirring constantly to remove lumps. When the mixture is smooth, add 1–2 parts of ammonium carbonate. This will bubble and turn the solution syrupy. Allow this to stand for about 30 minutes, then add between 4 and 8 parts of water, depending on what consistency you want. Finally, tint the paint to your chosen color with powder pigment dissolved in a little water. Casein distemper should be applied with a bristle brush, but do not allow the paint to dry on the brush. Wash brushes in soapy water after use.

GESSO

Gesso is a hard, off-white substance that resembles plaster and is used as a base for tortoiseshelling, gilding, or painting. Traditionally made from rabbit-skin glue and whiting, it is now also available in a highly effective acrylic-based, cold liquid form, which can be used as a primer for canvas and wood.

To make traditional gesso, you will need rabbit-skin granules, available from good-quality art supply stores. Soak the granules in water overnight following the recommended quantities, then heat the swollen granules in a double boiler until they dissolve, being careful not to let the solution boil. Remove from the heat and allow to cool to a jelly. The jelly should split when pressed between thumb and finger. Mix up to half the same amount of whiting, stirring constantly, until the warm gesso has the consistency of light cream.

To apply gesso, heat it gently without boiling and apply the first coat with a stiff brush or rag. After a few minutes, apply a second coat at right-angles to the first. You will need four or five coats, each applied in opposite directions, bearing in mind that each succeeding coat will take longer to dry. Reheat the gesso each time you use it. When the final coat is dry, polish the gesso with very fine sandpaper using a circular motion. The surface should appear completely matte when viewed from the front, but a high sheen should be visible if you look along it towards the light.

Suppliers of paints, oils, varnishes, glazes, and brushes

USA
Arch
407 Jackson Street
San Francisco,
CA 94111
415 433 2724
mail order available

Art Seller
435 University Avenue
San Diego, CA 92103
415 295 0928

Art Things
2 Annapolis Street
Annapolis, MD 21401
301 268 3520

Arthur Brown and
  Bros., Inc
2 West 46th Street
New York, NY 10036
212 575 5555

Ashley House
  Wallcoverings Inc.
1838 West Broadway
Vancouver, BC V6J JY9
604 734 4131

Benjamin Moore &
  Company
51 Chestnut Ridge Road
Montvale, NJ 07645
800 344 0400

Binder's Art Center
P.O. Box 52815
Atlanta, GA 30355
404 885 1200
mail order available

Carter Sexton
5308 Laurel Canyon
  Blvd.
North Hollywood,
LA 41607
818 763 5050
fax 818 763 5050

Charrette Favor Ruhl
31 Olympia Avenue
Woburn, MA 01888
800 367 3729
mail order available

Co-op Artists Materials
P.O. Box 53097
Atlanta, GA 30355
404 497 9919
mail order available

Cohasset Colonials
38 Parker Avenue
Cohasset, MA 02025
617 383 0010
mail order available

Colorcrafters
5907 Emilie Road
Levittown, PA 19057
215 946 6630

Creative Merchandizers
785 Andersen Drive
San Rafael, CA 94901
415 453 7676

David Art Center
2629 Edenborn Avenue
Metairie, LA 70002
504 888 3630

Diamond Vogel/Kormac
  Paints
1201 Osage Street
Denver, CO 80204
303 534 5191

Finnaren and Haley Inc.
2329 Haverford Road
Ardmore, PA 19003
215 649 5000

Flax Artist's and
  Drafting Supplies
1460 North High Drive
Atlanta, GA 30318
404 32 7200
mail order available

Flax's
1699 Market Street
San Francisco,
CA 94103
415 552 2355

Guiry's Inc.
2468 South Co Blvd.
Denver, CO 80222
303 758 8244
fax 303 756 3545
mail order available

H.G. Daniels
2543 West 6th Street
Los Angeles, CA 90057
800 866 6601

H.G. Daniels
1844 India Street
San Diego, CA 92101
800 866 6601
fax 800 655 0271
mail order available

Janovic Plaza
1150 Third Avenue
New York, NY 10022
212 772 1400

Janovic Plaza
30-35 Thomson Avenue
Long Island City,
NY 11101
718 392 3999

Johnson Paint Company
355 Newbury Street
Boston, MA 02115
617 536 4838/4244
fax 617 536 8832

KC Art Supplies
209 Court Street
Brooklyn, NY 11201
718 852 1271

Koenig Philidelphia Art
25 South 8th Street
Philidelphia, PA 19106
215 627 6655

Kurfees Coating Inc.
210 East Market Street
Louisville, KY 40202
502 584 0151

Loew-Cornell Inc.
563 Chestnut Avenue
Teaneck, NJ 0766 2490
201 836 7070
fax 2901 836 8110

Paint Magic
2426 Fillmore Street
San Francisco,
CA 94115
415 292 7780

Pearl Paint Company
308 Canal Street
New York, NY 10013
212 431 7932

Sam Flax
12 West 20th Street
New York, NY 10011
212 620 3038

Sherwin Williams
101 Prospect Avenue
Cleveland, OH 44115
216 566 2000

South Street Art Supply
515 Spring Garden
  Street
Philadelphia, PA 19123
215 923 2115

Standard Brands
3 Masonic Avenue
San Francisco,
CA 94118
415 922 4003

Stencil World
1456 Second Avenue,
  Box 175
New York, NY 10021
212 517 7164

Texas Art Supply
2001 Montrose
Houston, TX 77006
713 526 5221
mail order available

The Art Store
7200 West Beverly Blvd.
Los Angeles, CA 90036
213 933 9284

The Art Store
5301 Broadway
Oakland,
CA 94618
415 658 2787

The Art Store
44 South Raymond
Pasadena, CA 91105
818 795 4985

Wolf Paints
Janovic Plaza
771 Ninth Avenue
New York, NY 10019
212 245 3241

CANADA
Day's Painting Supplies
10733 104 Ave. N.W.
Edmonton, AB TDJ 3K1
403 426 4848

Hartmann House
  Products
4422 Wellington Road
Nanaimo
British Columbia,
Canada V9T 2H3
800 665 2833
mail order available

New York Paint and
  Wallpaper
1704 St. Clair Avenue
  West
Toronto, ON M6N 1J1
416 656 2233

Index

Acknowledgments

The Author would like to thank the following for their support and assistance:

Specialist painters:
Helen Shakespeare
42 Listria Park
London N16
Tel: 0802 440316

Alice Williams
29 Gathorne Road
London N22
Tel: 0973 390485

Clare Bailey
182 Ladbroke Grove
London W10
Tel: 0181 968 7601

Peter Thwaites
Garden Flat
3 Belsize Park Gardens
London NW3
Tel: 0171 586 0441

Stylist
(London Projects)
Ruth Delaney
184 Westbourne Park Road
London W11
Tel: 0171 229 1042

Paints and Materials
Craig and Rose Plc
172 Leith Walk
Edinburgh
Tel: 0131 554 1131

Daler-Rowney Ltd
P.O. Box 10
Bracknell
Berkshire
Tel: 01344 424 621

Furniture and Accessories
(London Projects)
McCloud & Co.
269 Wandsworth Bridge Road
London SW6
Tel: 0171 371 7151

Jinan
17 Golden Square
London W1
Tel: 0171 434 3464

Themes and Variations
231 Westbourne Grove
London W11
Tel: 0171 727 5531

Carolyn Quartermaine
Chez Joseph
26 Sloane Street
London SW1
Tel: 0171 245 9493

Thanks also to everyone at Conran Octopus for their profound patience; to Patrick Baty at Papers and Paints for his technical expertise; to James Mortimer and Peter Aprahamian for their wonderful photographs; and to everyone else who has worked with me and helped me, in particular, Suzanne Sundara-Garuda, Emily Phillips, Flick Stainthorpe, Christian Corgier, Scott Cunningham and Marie-France Boyer.

This book owes a very special debt of gratitude to Min Hogg, without whom I might never have made my first faltering steps into the world of interiors. It is dedicated to Elizabeth Herbert.

The Publisher would like to thank Jane Royston, Sarah Widdecombe, Penelope Cream and Helen Green.

The publisher would like to thank the following photographers and organizations for their kind permission to reproduce the photographs in this book:

2 Fritz von der Schulenburg (Designer: Mimmi O'Connell/Painter: Juliette Mole)/The Interior Archive; 4 Christopher Simon Sykes (Celia Lyttleton)/The Interior Archive; 6 Richard Waite (Interior Design by Louise Cotier)/Arcaid; 8 Mads Mogensen; 9 Martyn Thompson (Kate Constable); 10 above left Martyn Thompson (Kate Constable); 10-11 Polly Wreford/Homes & Gardens/Robert Harding Syndication; 12 Christopher Simon Sykes (Maxine de la Falaise)/The Interior Archive; 13 Tim Street-Porter (Architect: Ricardo Legorreta); 14 above Martyn Thompson (Kate Constable); 14 below Rene Stoeltie; 15 Tim Clinch/The Interior Archive; 16 above left Martyn Thompson (Kate Constable); 16 right Jean-Pierre Godeaut (Ungaro); 16 below left Paul Ryan/International Interiors; 17 Simon McBride; 18 T. Jeanson/SIP; 19 Ianthe Ruthven; 20 Dennis Krukowski; 21 Fritz von der Schulenburg/The Interior Archive; 22 Christopher Simon Sykes/The Interior Archive; 23 Dennis Krukowski; 24 Fritz von der Schulenburg/The Interior Archive; 25 John Hall; 26 above left Martyn Thompson (Kate Constable); 26 below left Henry Wilson (Leslie Goring)/The Interior Archive; 26-7 Rene Stoeltie; 27 right Fritz von der Schulenburg/The Interior Archive; 28 below left Mads Mogensen; 28-9 Christian Sarramon; 29 right Marie-Pierre Morel (Stylist: Catherine Ardouin)/Marie Claire Maison; 30 Pascal Chevalier (Michel Klein)/Agence Top; 31 above left Pascal Chevalier (Michel Klein)/Agence Top; 31 above right Martyn Thompson; 31 below Ingalill Snitt; 32 left Simon McBride; 32-3 Mads Mogensen; 33 right Fritz von der Schulenburg/The Interior Archive; 34 above Ingalill Snitt; 34 below Michael Freeman (Mable Dodge Luhan House); 35 left Christian Sarramon; 35 right Ingalill Snitt; 36 left Martyn Thompson (Kate Constable); 36-7 Scott Frances/Esto; 37 above Fritz von der Schulenburg (Painter: Ari Shand)/The Interior Archive; 38-9 Elizabeth Whiting & Associates; 38 below left David Phelps; 39 above right Tim Beddow/The Interior Archive; 39 below right Geoffrey Frosh; 40-1 Jean-François Jaussaud (Ines de la Fressange)/SIP; 42 Hotze Eisma; 42-3 Verne Fotografie; 43 Tim Street-Porter (Gregory Evans); 44 Tim Goffe; 45 Tim Street-Porter (Artist: Nancy Kintisch/Decorator: Jarrett and Hedborg); 46-7 John Hall; 46 above left Tim Street-Porter (Artist: Nancy Kintisch/Decorator: Jarrett and Hedborg); 46 below left Derry Moore/The Interior Archive; 47 David Phelps; 48-9 Christophe Dugied/Marine Archang; 48 above left Tim Street-Porter (Artist: Nancy Kintisch/Decorator: Jarrett and Hedborg); 48 below left Fritz von der Schulenburg (Christophe Gollut)/The Interior Archive; 50

Polly Wreford (Artist: Adrian Rose)/Homes & Gardens/Robert Harding Syndication; 51 above Polly Wreford/Homes & Gardens/Robert Harding Syndication; 51 below Marie-Pierre Morel (Stylist: Catherine Ardouin)/Marie Claire Maison; 52 above Tim Street-Porter (Artist: Nancy Kintisch/Decorator: Jarrett and Hedborg); 52 above right Hotze Eisma (Miguel Goldschmidt)/V.T. Wonen; 52 below right Todd Eberle; 52 below left Dennis Krukowski; 53 Richard Davies/Homes & Gardens/Robert Harding Syndication; 54 above left Tim Street-Porter (Artist: Nancy Kintisch/Decorator: Jarrett and Hedborg); 54 below left Sølvi Dos Santos; 56 above Tim Street-Porter; 56 below Elizabeth Whiting & Associates; 57 Steve Gross and Sue Daley (Abby Blackwald); 58 above left Tim Street-Porter (Artist: Nancy Kintisch/Decorator: Jarrett and Hedborg); 58 below left Chris Drake (John Plummer)/Homes & Gardens; 58-9 Tim Beddow/The Interior Archive; 60-1 Simon Upton/Elizabeth Whiting & Associates ; 60 left Steve Gross and Sue Daley (Vezna and Jim Tozzi); 61 above right David Parmiter/Homes & Gardens/Robert Harding Syndication; 61 Below right Hotze Eisma; 62 above right Fritz von der Schulenburg (Chesterton)/The Interior Archive; 62 above left Tim Street-Porter (Artist: Nancy Kintisch/Decorator: Hedborg and Jarrett); 62 below left Simon Wheeler; 63 Jan Baldwin (Andrew Mortada); 64-5 above Jean-Pierre Godeaut; 64 below left Ianthe Ruthven; 64-5 below Ianthe Ruthven; 65 right Martyn Thompson; 66 below left Wayne Vincent (Designer: Lesley Saddington)/The Interior Archive; 66 above left Tim Street-Porter (Artist: Nancy Kintisch/Decorator: Jarrett and Hedborg); 66-7 Paul Ryan/International Interiors; 67 above right Jean-Pierre Godeaut (Lisa Lovatt Smith); 67 below right Marianne Majerus; 68 above Fritz von der Schulenburg (Painter: Ari Shand) The Interior Archive; 68 above left Tim Street-Porter (Artist: Nancy Kintisch/Decorator: Jarrett and Hedborg); 68 below left Scott Frances/Esto; 68 below right John Hall; 69 Nicolas Tosi (Stylist: J. Borgeaud)/Marie Claire Maison; 70-1 James Mortimer (Ruth Harjula)/The World of Interiors; 71 above Studio Brackrock; 71 below Mark Bolton (Debbie Creed)/Homes & Gardens; 72 above left Tim Street-Porter (Artist: Nancy Kintisch/Decorators: Jarrett and Hedborg); 72 below left Hotze Eisma; 72-3 Jean-Pierre Godeaut; 73 above right Michael Freeman; 73 below left Eric Morin; 74-5 Todd Eberle; 74 below left Jean-Pierre Godeaut (Designer: Manuel Mestre); 74 above left Nadia Mackenzie; 75 right Nadia Mackenzie; 76 Peter Woloszynski/The Interior Archive; 77 Tim Street-Porter (Tom Beeton); 78 above left Tim Street-Porter (Tom Beeton); 78 below Christopher Simon Sykes (Maxine de la Falaise)/The Interior Archive; 79 Steve Gross and Sue Daley; 81 above Todd Eberle; 81 below Jean-François Jaussaud; 82 Crown; 83 Tim Beddow (D. Rombeaut)/The Interior Archive;

85 James Mortimer/The World of Interiors; 86 Steve Gross and Sue Daley (Hasbrouk House); 90 Steve Gross and Sue Daley; 92 Peter Woloszynski/The Interior Archive; 96 Tim Clinch/The Interior Archive; 99 Simon Brown/The Interior Archive; 100 Hans Zeegers (Stylist: Linda Loenen)/Ariadne; 101 Fritz von der Schulenburg (Designer: Mimmi O'Connell/Painter: Juliette Mole)/The Interior Archive; 102 above left Jean-Pierre Godeaut (Dimitr Xanthoulis); 102-3 Ianthe Ruthven; 104 Nadia Mackenzie; 106 Mads Mogensen; 107 Steve Gross and Sue Daley (Ryan Gainey); 108 Pascal Chevalier/Agence Top; 110-11 Camera Press; 112 T. Jeanson/SIP; 114-5 Peter Woloszynski/The Interior Archive; 116 Trevor Richards/Homes & Gardens/Robert Harding Syndication; 118 Rene Stoeltie; 119 Simon McBride; 134-5 Peter Aprahamian/The World of Interiors; 142-3 James Mortimer/The World of Interiors; 144 Peter Aprahamian; 145 Peter Aprahamian; 146-51 Peter Aprahamian/The World of Interiors; 156-7 James Mortimer/The World of Interiors; 160 James Mortimer/The World of Interiors; 161 Christophe Dugied/Marine Archang; 162 above right Fritz von der Schulenburg/The Interior Archive; 163 Andreas von Einsiedal/Homes & Gardens/Robert Harding Syndication; 164-5 Fritz von der Schulenburg/The Interior Archive; 165 right Couturier/Archipress; 166 right Simon Brown (Justin Meath Baker); 168 right Hotze Eisma; 169 Christopher Simon Sykes (Celia Lyttleton)/The Interior Archive; 170 above Tim Street-Porter (Michael Anderson); 170 below Hotze Eisma; 171 Tim Street-Porter (Michael Anderson); 172 right Jean-Pierre Godeaut (Ecco Musée, Alsace); 172 above left David Phelps; 174 right Jean-Pierre Godeaut; 174 centre Nadia Mackenzie; 174 left Christian Sarramon/SIP; 174 below right Tripelon-Jarry/Agence Top; 175 above David Phelps; 175 below left Jane Gifford/Country Homes & Interiors/Robert Harding Syndication; 175 below right Michael Freeman; 176 below Hotze Eisma; 176 left Jean-François Jaussaud; 178 above Elle Decoration (Hannah Lewis & Sue Parker); 178 centre Jean-François Jaussaud; 178 below Richard Felber; 179 above Paul Ryan/International Interiors; 179 centre Hotze Eisma; 179 below Tom Leighton/Options/Robert Harding Syndication; 180 above Christophe Dugied/Marine Archang; 180 right Fritz von der Schulenburg (Painter: Ari Shand)/The Interior Archive; 181 above right Fritz von der Schulenburg (Painter: Ari Shand)/The Interior Archive; 181 above left Nadia Mackenzie; 181 below left Michael Freeman; 182 Andreas von Einsiedel/Homes & Gardens/Robert Harding Syndication.

THE FOLLOWING PHOTOGRAPHS WERE SPECIALLY TAKEN FOR CONRAN OCTOPUS:
Peter Aprahamian: 122, 123, 130-3, 136-7, 138-41, 158-9.
James Mortimer: 1, 54-5, 120-1, 124-7, 128-9, 152-3, 154-5.
Patrick McLeavey: 183-6, 188-9, 191-2, 194, 200.